The Business Analyst as Strategist

Translating Business Strategies
into Valuable Solutions

The Business Analyst as Strategist

Translating Business Strategies into Valuable Solutions

Kathleen B. Hass, PMP

MANAGEMENTCONCEPTS

MANAGEMENTCONCEPTS

8230 Leesburg Pike, Suite 800
Vienna, VA 22182
703.790.9595
Fax: 703.790.1371
www.managementconcepts.com

Printed in the United States of America

Library of Congress Cataloging-in-Publication Data

Hass, Kathleen B.
The business analyst as strategist / Kathleen B. Hass.
   p. cm. -- (Business analysis essential library)
 Includes bibliographical references and index.
 ISBN 978-1-56726-209-4 (alk. paper)
    1. Business analysts. 2. Strategic planning. 3. Information technology--Management.
    4. Business planning. I. Title.
 HD69.B87H368 2008
 658.4'012--dc22

                                                                2007037989

10   9   8   7   6   5   4   3   2   1

About the Author

Kathleen Hass is the Project Management and Business Analysis Practice Leader for Management Concepts. Ms. Hass is a prominent presenter at industry conferences and is an author and lecturer in strategic project management and business analysis disciplines. Her expertise includes leading technology and software-intensive projects, building and leading strategic project teams, and conducting program management for large, complex engagements. Ms. Hass has more than 25 years of experience in project management and business analysis, including project portfolio management implementation, project office creation and management, business process reengineering, IT applications development and technology deployment, project management and business analysis training and mentoring, and requirements management. Ms. Hass has managed large, complex projects in the airline, telecommunications, retail, and manufacturing industries and in the U.S. federal government.

Ms. Hass' consulting experience includes engagements with multiple agencies within the federal government, such as USDA, USGS, NARA, and an agency within the intelligence community, as well as industry engagements at Colorado Springs Utilities, Toyota Financial Services, Toyota Motor Sales, the Salt Lake Organizing Committee for the 2002 Olympic Winter Games, Hilti US Inc., The SABRE Group, Sulzer Medica, and Qwest Communications. Client services have included maturity assessments, project quality and risk assessment, project launches, troubled project recovery, risk management, and implementation of program management offices, strategic planning, and project portfolio management processes.

Ms. Hass earned a B.A. in business administration with summa cum laude honors from Western Connecticut University.

Table of Contents

Part II – Using Portfolio Management to Achieve Strategic Goals

Preface

The Business Analysis Essential Library is a series of books that each cover a separate and distinct area of business analysis. The business analyst ensures that there is a strong business focus for the projects that emerge as a result of the fierce, competitive nature and rapid rate of change of business today. Within both private industry and government agencies, the business analyst is becoming the central figure in leading major change initiatives. This library is designed to explain the emerging role of the business analyst and present contemporary business analysis practices (the what), supported by practical tools and techniques to enable the application of the practices (the how).

Current books in the series are:

+ *Professionalizing Business Analysis: Breaking the Cycle of Challenged Projects*

+ *The Business Analyst as Strategist: Translating Business Strategies into Valuable Solutions*

+ *Unearthing Business Requirements: Elicitation Tools and Techniques*

+ *Getting it Right: Business Requirement Analysis Tools and Techniques*

+ *The Art and Power of Facilitation: Running Powerful Meetings*

  ✦ *From Analyst to Leader: Elevating the Role of the Business Analyst*

Check the Management Concepts website, www.managementconcepts.com/pubs, for updates to this series.

About This Book

An organization's ability to achieve strategic goals through programs and supporting projects depends on its ability to establish a future vision, set strategic goals, select the most valuable projects, and then execute flawlessly. Organizational strategic alignment is achieved by converting strategic plans and goals into a valuable portfolio of programs and supporting projects, as depicted in Figure I-1. Strategic project leaders and project teams execute the project plans to meet objectives and deliver project outcomes, adding value to the organization.

Figure I-1—Organizational Strategic Alignment

Strategic Plans & Goals Established

Program Portfolio Selected

Supporting Projects Launched

Core Strategic Project Teams Execute

Strategic Goals

Programs

Projects

Activities—Teams—Results

Valuable Project Outcomes Drive Achievement of Strategic Goals

Organizational Maturity
Professional Business Analysts and Project Managers

As the role of the business analyst evolves and matures, senior business analysts will emerge as the key individuals in the organization who have the depth of business acumen and technological proficiency to serve as both business and technology experts. In this capacity, business analysts will become involved in an array of activities designed to devise a strategy to reach the organization's future business vision by achieving strategic goals.

As the business analyst elevates into a leadership role as the business and technology strategist, he or she serves the executive team by facilitating, informing, and enabling the most favorable business decisions during the strategic planning and enterprise analysis phases of the business solution life cycle (BSLC). This book examines the emerging critical role of the business analyst during these first two phases of the BSLC, depicted in Figure I-2.

The business analyst, in collaboration with project and portfolio managers, provides the executive leadership team with the information, processes, tools, and capability to make the best decisions regarding:

- The future vision of the organization

- Strategic plans and goals designed to realize the vision

- Strategic measures to gauge progress along the way

- Programs and supporting projects that facilitate the most valuable change initiatives

- Organizational capabilities that can achieve project objectives in the fastest time to market, to realize project benefits at the earliest possible moment

- Organizational change management strategies for implementing new business solutions and optimizing returns on project investments

Figure I-2—The Business Solution Life Cycle

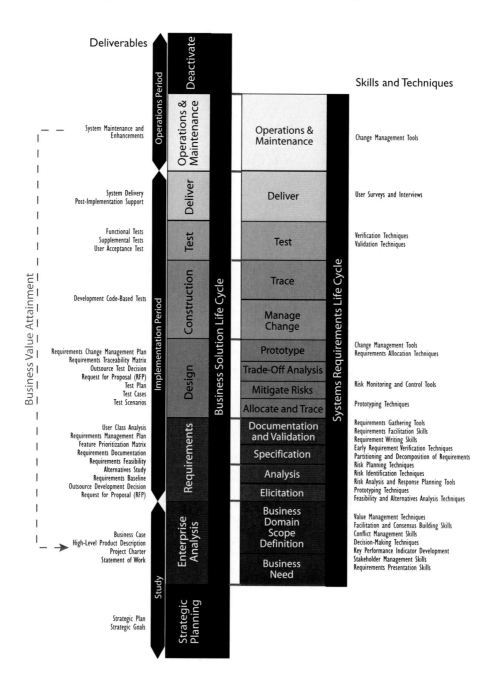

The knowledge, skills, and techniques needed by the business analyst to conduct pre-project business analysis activities are referred to collectively as *enterprise analysis*. The International Institute of Business Analysis (IIBA) is currently drafting *A Guide to the Business Analysis Body of Knowledge (BABOK™ Guide)*, which defines *enterprise analysis* as follows:[1]

> *Enterprise analysis is the knowledge area of the Business Analysis Body of Knowledge (BABOK™) that describes the business analysis activities that take place for organizations to (1) identify business opportunities, (2) build their business architecture framework, and (3) determine the optimum project investment path for the enterprise, including implementation of new business and technical system solutions.*

> *The enterprise analysis knowledge area consists of the collection of pre-project activities for capturing the future view of the business to provide context to project requirements elicitation and solution design for a given initiative and/or for long-term planning. In some large complex organizations this work is treated as an investigative, feasibility, or business architecture endeavor and is managed as a stand-alone project.*

> *During enterprise analysis activities, the business requirements for future project investments are identified and documented. Business requirements are defined as high-level statements of the goals, objectives, or needs of the enterprise. They describe such things as the reasons why a project is initiated, the things that the project will achieve, and the metrics which will be used to measure its success.*

---

[1] The International Institute of Business Analysis, *A Guide to the IIBA Body of Knowledge, Draft Material for Review and Feedback*, Release 1.6 Draft, 2006, http://download.theiiba.org/files/BOKV1_6.pdf (accessed August 3, 2007).

As chairperson of the committee that drafted this enterprise analysis chapter of the *BABOK™ Guide*, the author is very familiar with the subject of enterprise analysis. This book builds further on the concepts presented in that chapter of the *BABOK™ Guide*, and provides additional information, tools, techniques, and best practices. Figure I-3 is a standard flow chart of basic enterprise analysis activities.

Figure I-3—Enterprise Analysis Activities

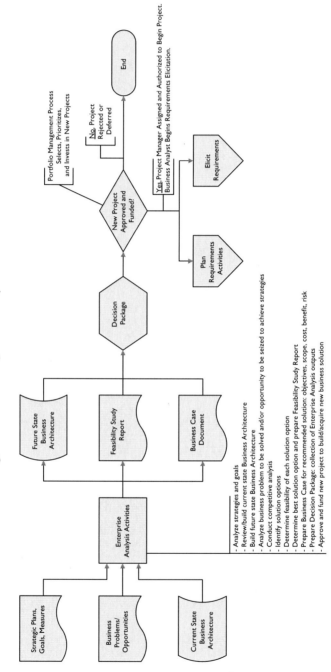

Part I

The Business Analyst's Role in Strategic Planning and Enterprise Analysis

To evolve from an internal business and technology consultant to a member of the executive leadership team, the business analyst must be equipped to make project selection decisions that align with greater organizational strategies. To make these decisions, the business analyst must fully understand both strategic planning processes and portfolio management practices that take place in the enterprise analysis phase of the business solution life cycle (BSLC). Part I defines the first two phases of the BSLC—the strategic planning phase and the enterprise analysis phase—and focuses on the role of the business analyst during those phases.

The executive leadership team begins to set the stage for strategic change during the strategic planning phase of the BSLC. Chapter 1 defines strategic planning, discusses why it is needed, and explores the business analyst's role in planning activities.

After planning, strategies are translated into operational terms through a portfolio of programs and supporting projects during the enterprise analysis phase of the BSLC. Chapter 2 defines portfolio analysis and portfolio management, and discusses the emerging role of the business analyst in those activities.

Chapter 1

The Emerging Role of the Business Analyst in Strategic Planning

In This Chapter:

- Strategic Planning in Organizations Today
- The Business Analyst's Role in Strategic Planning

To respond to the never-ending demand for new products and services, executives everywhere are adopting professional business analysis practices to improve their ability to establish and execute strategy. At the strategic level, business analysis best practices aim to formulate the best business strategies, select projects to achieve those strategies, and increase the value project deliverables bring to the business.

Strategic Planning in Organizations Today

Executives are learning that to set the most favorable vision and strategy, they need to dedicate a significant portion of their time and energy to the formulation, execution, continuous monitoring, and refinement of strategy. To formulate and execute a well-formed strategy, leadership teams must anticipate market needs, exploit opportunities, identify threats, and make decisions that support their corporate objectives—a tall order.

For this discussion, it is appropriate to look to the foremost experts in strategy formulation, execution, and measurement, Robert

S. Kaplan and David P. Norton. Robert Kaplan is the Marvin Bower Professor of Leadership Development at Harvard Business School and cofounder and chairman of BSCol (Balanced Scorecard Collaborative). David Norton is cofounder, president, and CEO of BSCol. Kaplan and Norton have coauthored several publications on strategy, including *The Balanced Scorecard: Translating Strategy Into Action* (Harvard Business School Publishing, 1996), *The Strategy-Focused Organization: How Balanced Scorecard Companies Thrive in the New Business Environment* (Harvard Business School Publishing, 2000), and three articles on the balanced scorecard in the *Harvard Business Review*. Through their efforts, executives are gaining knowledge of how to combine the expertise and principles of the strategy-focused organization with corporate performance management methods and techniques. Their theories, recommendations, and techniques appear throughout Chapters 1 and 2.

So how are strategies formulated today, and what is the role of the business analyst? The executive leadership team alone cannot effect the transition to a strategically focused organization. The *information, process, tools, and facilitation* that enable the organization to shift focus and become strategically driven are largely provided through the efforts of senior business analysts.

Before setting strategies, the leadership team needs to have up-to-date information regarding the competitive environment within which their business operates. Strategic planning processes begin by conducting research, competitive analyses, benchmark studies, and the like. The business analyst provides critical information to the executive team as an input to strategic planning discussions. In addition to critical information, the business analyst and senior managers also develop and use processes and tools during facilitated strategy meetings, and later during project selection and prioritization sessions, as well as ongoing program and project reviews. Specific activities the business analyst performs to enable the leadership team to formulate and execute strategy fall into four categories:

- Conducting research and presenting findings

- Establishing strategic goals and themes

- Selecting change initiatives

- Measuring progress over time

Conducting Research and Presenting Findings

For business requirements and goals to convert into innovative solutions that truly reflect the needs of the business and bring wealth to the organization, strategic planning and strategic goal-setting processes alone are not sufficient. To strongly link project selection to the organizational vision, those activities must be combined with business analysis—a comprehensive examination of business needs, environmental considerations, business opportunities, and business problems.

To establish the best direction in terms of vision, strategy, and goals, business analysts provide executives with an understanding of the current state of the industry and of critical market threats. In addition, analysts determine the competitiveness of their organization's products and services, any impending innovations on the horizon, national and global marketplace pressures, and the current state of their business processes, organizational capabilities, and supporting technology. The business analyst may also conduct a competitive analysis to determine the current state of the organization in relationship to its competition, or a benchmark study of organizational processes and practices used by leaders in the industry.

After studying industry trends outside the organization, the business analyst turns inward to conduct an analysis of the organization relative to its competition. The business analyst then typically prepares a report describing study methods and results, proposing various business problems and opportunities for consideration, and suggesting ways the organization might close the gap with competitors. This report may include information garnered from:

+ Investigating, comparing, and contrasting the organization's current strategy versus industry trends, marketplace pressures, and competitive threats

+ Assessing the current state of the organization's technology structure, and strategies to ensure that structure aligns with the business vision

+ Identifying current business problems and determining their root causes

+ Assessing whether current internal processes and organizational capabilities sustain the current competitive advantage and are profitable and efficient, and whether they may help seize new competitive advantages

Establishing Strategic Goals and Themes

The executive leadership team typically defines the organization's future in terms of vision, mission, and strategic goals. Norton suggests that in order to execute strategies organizations must convert strategic goals and objectives into *strategic themes*.[1] Once the senior business analyst demonstrates to the executive leadership team that he or she has a grasp of the critical information needed to devise future strategies, the senior team then may enlist the business analyst to facilitate strategy-forming sessions to establish strategic goals and themes. Strategic themes reflect goals related to financial performance, customer value, business operations, and the capabilities of the workforce and other corporate assets. Refer to Table 1-1 for an understanding of the relationship between strategic goals and strategic themes.

Table 1-1—Strategic Goals and Themes

Strategic Goals	Strategic Themes
Reduce operating costs	Reduce operating costs through online customer ordering
Increase the number of high-value customers	Increase the number of high-value customers through mergers and acquisitions
Increase revenue per customer	Increase revenue per customer by adding to the products and services offered to each customer

Selecting Change Initiatives

Once strategic themes are fully developed, the next step is to use the themes to select and prioritize change initiatives needed to achieve the strategies set by the executive leadership team. Change initiatives are carried out through programs and supporting projects. *Projects make change happen.* Projects might include training and retooling the current workforce, developing new IT-enabled business systems, reengineering current business processes, or establishing new business units. Projects are accomplished through an effective portfolio management process, the subject of Chapter 2.

Measuring Progress Over Time

So how do we measure progress along the way? In addition to selecting and prioritizing strategic projects, business analysts need to convert strategic themes into an organized, actionable, measurable framework to provide a guidepost for measuring progress along the way. Norton and Kaplan introduced the corporate scorecard as a performance measurement technique in their book, *The Balanced Scorecard: Translating a Strategy into Action.*[2] Many organizations are developing corporate strategic scorecards to frame strategic themes and measure progress. As an outgrowth of the strategic plan, the business analyst facilitates the conversion of strategic themes into strategic scorecard elements—usually categorized into financial, customer service, internal operations, and learning/innovation groups—and helps executive leadership teams build the measures.[3]

Repeating the Planning Cycles

Strategic plans will change as the competitive landscape changes. Strategic goals, themes, and measures are dynamic as well. Therefore, the business analyst and senior managers meet with the executive leadership team repeatedly during ever-tighter planning cycles to rigorously monitor progress and make course corrections as necessary. The bar for adding business value is raised for every planning cycle as competition strengthens.

The executive team cannot perform these rigorous and time-consuming strategic planning activities without the help of senior business analysts who can bring together all the elements that go into good strategy and good execution. Elements include:

- The options and the relevant costs and benefits of proposed opportunities

- The project resource capacity and expertise needed to deliver a quality business solution

- The impacts of change initiatives on the organization as a whole and on specific business units

- Methods for measuring progress toward the expected business value

- Guidance for formulating a course of action and project-related direction in terms of goals and constraints

- Project reviews for ongoing management oversight and required course correction, including project termination, when warranted

- Measurement of the actual value added to the enterprise

The Business Analyst's Role in Strategic Planning

Not all business analysts are involved in all aspects of strategic planning. It is a complex and important process, and it should be entrusted to the most senior and expert business analysts. In many organizations, business analysts do not yet participate directly or even indirectly in strategic planning, although this trend is changing. More and more senior business analysts are invited into the boardroom to provide vital information to the strategic planning team. Even if an organization doesn't ask its business analysts to participate in the strategic planning process, business analysts and project managers should still focus on the organization's strategic goals to ensure that new initiatives fit into those long-term plans and to help build and manage the business case and other relevant information about new project opportunities.

To evolve from an internal business and technology consultant to a member of the executive leadership team, the senior business analyst needs to fully understand strategic planning processes and portfolio management practices to make project selection decisions that align with greater organizational strategies. The business analysis activities required to determine which projects are most likely to achieve business objectives are conducted during the enterprise analysis phase of the BSLC, introduced in Chapter 2.

Endnotes

1. David P. Norton presented "Project Balanced Scorecards—A Tool for Alignment, Teamwork and Results," at ProjectWorld & The World Congress for Business Analysts Conference in Orlando Florida on November 17, 2005. For more information about ProjectWorld & The World Congress for Business Analysts Conference, visit www.projectworld.com (accessed September 2007).

2. Robert Kaplan and David Norton. *The Balanced Scorecard: Translating a Strategy into Action*, 1996. Cambridge: Harvard Business School Press.

3. Ibid.

Chapter 2

The Emerging Role of the Business Analyst in Portfolio Management

In This Chapter:

- Strategy Execution
- Why Portfolio Management?
- Defining Portfolio Management
- The Portfolio Management Process
- Portfolio Management at the Project Level
- The Role of the Program Management Office
- Implementation Strategies
- Challenges
- Best Practices

As discussed in Chapter 1, strategic planning is the process of defining the mission and long-range objectives of an organization. It focuses the executive team on the organization's reason for being and lays the groundwork for the organization to make the most worthwhile investments to bring about desired changes. The scarcity of resources and time-to-market considerations force organizations to choose which improvements and innovations to invest in to align change initiatives with strategies. The challenge is to learn how to invest in those ideas that will bring *the most value to the organization, the fastest, with the least risk.*

In our global economy, there is a growing need to decrease the time it takes to make an informed decision. In other words, there is a need to improve the organization's *decision velocity*. Determining the most valuable candidate projects, however, requires some degree of analysis and planning. These analysis and planning activities occur within the enterprise analysis phase of the business solution life cycle (BSLC), culminating in a decision to invest in the new initiative, defer investment, or reject the proposed initiative altogether.

This chapter first examines why strategy is difficult to execute and why portfolio management is becoming a critical business management practice, and then defines the business analyst's role in portfolio management activities.

Strategy Execution

After strategic goals, themes, and measures are in place, program and project teams execute plans to achieve strategies. As the executive leadership team becomes more adept at the processes used to select and manage a portfolio of valuable projects, the amount of time they spend monitoring and governing strategic projects increases substantially. Throughout the BSLC, the business analyst and project manager present information to the executive leadership team so they can continually monitor project cost, schedule, risk, and quality for funded strategic initiatives; make course corrections along the way; review proposals for new initiatives developed and presented using sophisticated professional business analysis practices; and measure the value of project outcomes for the enterprise after deployment.

Organizations that execute strategy well do it by making *strategy execution* a core competency. The most innovative brainchild or creative suggestion does not add value unless turned into valuable products and services. According to Norton, "Ideas are only powerful if you can execute."[1] Norton goes on to propose a five-step process to establish and execute well-formed strategies:

1. *Mobilize change through executive leadership*: execute and continually monitor progress toward achieving critical strategies

2. *Translate strategy into operational terms*: select and prioritize the most valuable projects through an effective portfolio management process

3. *Align the organization to the strategy*: allocate resources to highest priority strategic projects first

4. *Motivate to make strategy everyone's job*: communicate the right message to the right people, align performance measurements to strategies, and reward progress toward strategy execution

5. *Govern to make strategy a continual process*: monitor, implement corrective actions, and provide executive oversight for strategic projects.

Well-formed strategies are translated into operational terms through a portfolio of programs and supporting projects. Resources are allocated to the most strategic projects first, aligning the organization to the strategy. Strategic project teams are recognized and rewarded for the value their project outcomes bring to the organization. Ongoing project reviews by the portfolio management group facilitate course corrections and refinements along the way.

So, how well do Fortune 500 companies execute strategy? According to David Norton, less than 10 percent of successfully formulated strategies are effectively executed.[2]

- Eighty-five percent of executives spend less than one hour per month on strategy.

+ Ninety-five percent of employees do not understand their organization's strategy.

+ Sixty percent of organizations do not link strategies to the budget.

+ Seventy percent of organizations do not link strategies to incentives.

We can assume that an equally disturbing percentage of programs and supporting projects are not aligned to strategies.

Why is this the case in corporate America, the most sophisticated business environment in history? Why is it that contemporary corporations and public entities continue to invest heavily in information technology (IT) projects to improve business operations without confirming that their strategy is correct?

According to Norton, businesses don't take time to confirm their strategies because "they can't manage something they can't describe."[3] Norton presents the argument that businesses without confirmed strategies lack an effective framework for describing and executing a business strategy. For example, the chief financial officer (CFO) may have a well-known financial strategy and an established financial information framework, but the chief executive officer (CEO) and executive leadership team may not have a similar framework for describing their business strategy. This discrepancy may impact an overall strategic framework driving business decisions.

As organizations struggle to implement project portfolio management, they are executing their strategy. It is the portfolio management process that links strategy to projects that are designed to accomplish *strategy execution*.

Why Portfolio Management?

Year after year, organizations spend a considerable percentage of their budget on projects, most with significant IT components, with disappointing results.[4] CIOs are under constant pressure to reduce IT costs *and* add value to the bottom line through IT products and services. There is no shortage of ideas to improve IT performance, and CIOs are struggling to determine the best approaches. Some of these approaches include outsourcing, implementing layoffs, allocating costs to user groups, standardizing technical platforms, improving project management capabilities, building enterprise architectures, implementing data warehouses, and providing web-based processing. The list goes on and on. The trick is for CIOs to use the *best* strategies with the least risk and the highest payback.

Choosing Among Change-Management Alternatives

One way to know how to choose the right change initiatives is to better understand the value of financial improvement alternatives for organizations that rely on significant IT support. In 2004, Eugene Lukac, then a partner in CSC's Consulting Group (currently a Specialist Leader in Deloitte Consulting's Strategy & Operations practice), suggested using an analytical framework to understand options:[5]

To understand the relative value of financial improvement options for IT, one needs an analytical framework that is rigorous and complete. Under such a framework, the effective management of IT is understood to involve converting the IT budget into IT resources, translating IT resources into IT output, and delivering business value from that IT output.

Lukac goes on to say that in using this decision framework, management has three possible "levers" to maximize the financial performance of IT:

+ *Resource management.* Strategies to manage resources include outsourcing major parts of the work, reorganizing the structure to flatten the organization and reduce managerial and

administrative expenses, and ensuring an optimum mix of senior, mid-level, and junior staff members.

+ *Work management.* Strategies to manage the work include
standardizing technology platforms and applications, employing Six Sigma practices to improve efficiency, investing in
building high-performing teams, and separating projects from
services.

+ *Demand management.* Strategies to control the demand for IT
projects and services include *implementing rigorous portfolio
management techniques* that align IT plans with the business
strategic plans, ensure there is a sound return on IT project
investments, control requests for new products and services
from the business to IT, and minimize investments in low-
value projects.

Figure 2-1 depicts these levers.[6]

Figure 2-1—Three Levers to Maximize the Business Value of IT

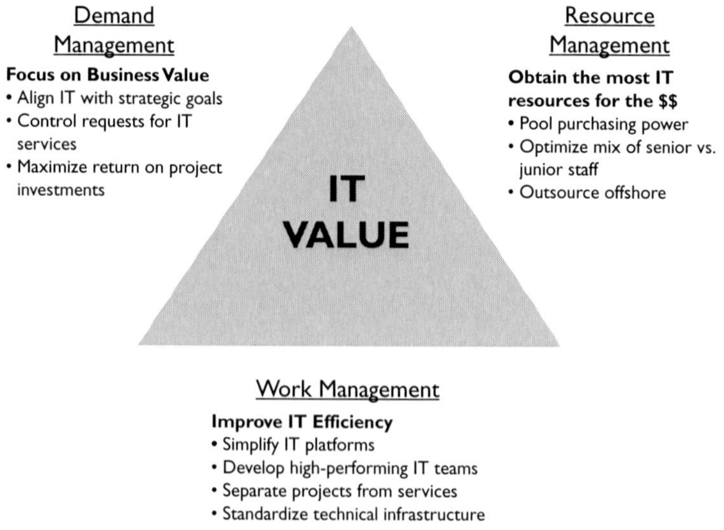

Demand
Management

Focus on Business Value
• Align IT with strategic goals
• Control requests for IT
  services
• Maximize return on project
  investments

**IT
VALUE**

Resource
Management

**Obtain the most IT
resources for the $$**
• Pool purchasing power
• Optimize mix of senior vs.
  junior staff
• Outsource offshore

Work Management

Improve IT Efficiency
• Simplify IT platforms
• Develop high-performing IT teams
• Separate projects from services
• Standardize technical infrastructure

This "three-lever" framework provides a useful structure for management to make decisions in each area, track progress toward achieving the strategies, and track cost savings. Lukac contends that demand management is much more powerful in terms of cost savings than work management, which in turn is more powerful than resource management. This makes sense because the primary value IT contributes to the organization is working on the most valuable projects and services to help capture the benefits of new business opportunities.

Recent evidence shows that organizations have a tendency to pull the resource management lever first, outsourcing their work, even though outsourcing is fraught with problems and risk. Lukac appropriately contends that this is a *worst practice*. Unintended ramifications of outsourcing abound, manifested by poor morale, loss of employee trust, and strategic changes that revert to insourcing because of disappointing cost-reduction results.

For example, a recent *CIO Magazine* article tells the story of the global financial services company JPMorgan Chase, which negotiated a $5 billion contract to outsource much of its IT. Over time, the company faced soaring costs and management teams that were distracted from key ventures because they were spending years preparing for the IT transition to the outsourcing vendor. Due to disappointing results, JPMorgan Chase recently decided to bring its IT resources back in-house, a decision that then necessitated more time and additional, significant costs.[7] It was a costly mistake to invest so much of the company's resources into outsourcing its IT programs.

All three levers should be used with the strongest emphasis on demand management, also known as portfolio management.

Why is Portfolio Management So Valuable?

Portfolio management—managing the demand for IT projects—provides the executive team with a system-wide view of projects across the enterprise, which makes it possible to make informed decisions about where to focus investments. To ensure that strategic goals create value, strategic goals and themes are translated into tangible programs and supporting projects through the portfolio management process. By aligning investments with projects that deliver outcomes to achieve strategic goals, portfolio management leads directly to improvements to the bottom line. The promise of project portfolio management is that for a given risk level, there is a specific mix of project investments that will achieve an optimal result.

Through portfolio management, project management is elevated to a strategic management process. The strategic goals, themes, and measures established during the planning process become the drivers of future projects. Decisions for project investments are no longer made within the functional silos that exist in most corporations and governmental agencies. The portfolio planning team is accountable for creating the right investment path for the enterprise and continually managing the portfolio of projects. This reduces duplication of effort, resolves inconsistencies in project objectives and scope, and optimizes the mix and scheduling of projects. Figure 2-2 depicts where portfolio management fits in a strategically focused organization.

As Figure 2-2 demonstrates, implementing portfolio management in an organization connects all employees to corporate strategies. Cross-functional project teams are treated as critical strategic resources. Individuals and teams are given clear, quantifiable performance expectations when they apply their knowledge, skills, tools, and techniques to create the project deliverables. Individual and team accountability is made clear.

As projects are launched, project managers are linked to strategic goals, themes, and measures. Project planning is focused on business-relevant outcomes. Project managers subdivide the overall project deliverables into smaller, measured outcomes until they are appropriate, individual assignments.

Figure 2-2—Strategic Project Management

Organizational Maturity
Environment for Project Success

Studies have been conducted to get a feel for how pervasive this new management process has become. In a 2005 study of 54 senior-level decision makers, 57.4 percent of the respondents reported that portfolio management had helped their organization improve focus and select the optimal projects. In addition, 70.4 percent said it had improved project alignment with their organization's overall strategy.[8]

The Business Analyst—Central to Effective Portfolio Management

Given the benefits of portfolio management, why aren't all organizations successfully implementing portfolio management strategies? The most significant reason is that organizations often lack the necessary management information and the focus required to address the burden of analysis to make informed decisions. Senior business analysts use an effective set of tools and processes to communicate actionable information to portfolio management team members who require this information to make the best project investments. Without the rigorous business analysis leading up to significant investments in programs and supporting projects, decisions are made based simply on intuition. This places the return on project investment at risk.

The business analyst plays a significant role in helping the executive leadership team translate business strategies into new business change initiatives. Ideally, the business analyst guides an array of enterprise analysis activities that lead up to project selection and prioritization. The following section takes a more detailed look at the portfolio management process to further define the critical role of the business analyst.

Defining Portfolio Management

Project investment portfolio management aims to achieve the maximum return on project investments—much like a financial portfolio aims to achieve the maximum return on financial investments. According to the Federal CIO Council, portfolio management involves five key objectives:[9]

+ *Defining goals and objectives*—clearly articulating what the portfolio is expected to achieve. Aligning the portfolio goals to the strategic goals.

+ *Understanding, accepting, and making tradeoffs*—determining how much to invest in one thing as opposed to something else.

+ *Identifying, eliminating, minimizing, and diversifying risk*—selecting a mix of investments that will avoid undue risk, will not exceed acceptable risk tolerance levels, and will spread risks across projects and initiatives to minimize adverse impacts.

+ *Monitoring portfolio performance*—understanding the progress that the portfolio is making toward the achievement of the goals and objectives.

+ *Achieving a desired objective*—having confidence that the desired outcome will likely be achieved given the aggregate investments.

Let us examine the portfolio management activities that support these objectives.

The Portfolio Management Process

Using expert facilitation, senior business analysts define the process the portfolio management team will follow and ensure that all team members agree to it. Figure 2-3 provides a typical portfolio management process flow chart.

The portfolio management process should be as simple and straightforward as possible. Process components typically include:

+ *Project proposal*—submitting a new project idea for consideration. From strategic plans and goals, the senior business analyst facilitates a small team of business and technology experts to draft portfolio investment objectives either as proposed solutions to business problem or as plans to seize new business opportunities. Then the expert team identifies potential project approaches and analyzes the feasibility of each option before drafting a business case for the most feasible option.

+ *Project approval*—reviewing, selecting, and prioritizing a proposed project. The portfolio management team makes adjustments to the portfolio if a new, approved project is a higher priority than current active projects. It may be necessary to reallocate resources from an active project, or even shut the active project down temporarily.

Figure 2-3—Portfolio Management Process Flow Chart

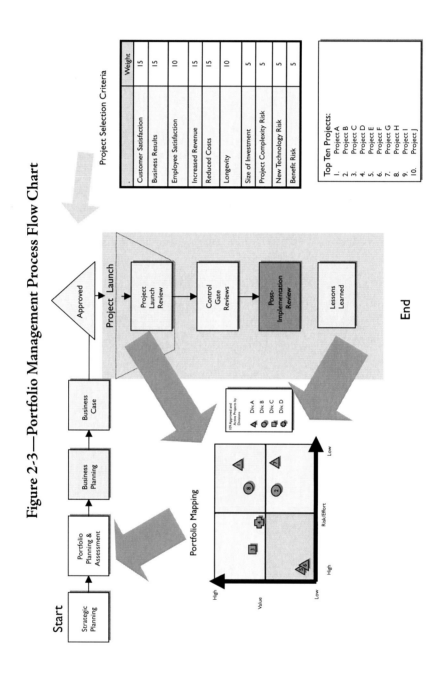

+ *Resource allocation*—allocating resources to high-priority projects first. The portfolio management team ensures that resources are properly allocated. Project resources are *finite* strategic assets—they can reach capacity and run out. Management must ensure that these vital corporate assets are deployed appropriately.

+ *Program reviews*—conducting control gate reviews of ongoing projects. The portfolio management team conducts ongoing control gate reviews to revalidate the business case, review current estimates of cost and time, validate or refine the project priority, and make a go/no-go decision about funding the project for the next major phase. Phase-based funding—the practice of funding only the next phase rather than the entire project—is becoming an essential risk-mitigation strategy in the quest to manage project portfolios.

+ *Project portfolio assessment*—reviewing, assessing, and prioritizing the entire portfolio of projects. The portfolio management team conducts a periodic assessment of the entire portfolio of projects to revisit, reaffirm, or make adjustments to the portfolio of projects as events occur, competitive advances emerge, technology moves forward, and business strategies change.

+ *Data management*—storing, maintaining, and reporting information about the portfolio. The portfolio management team needs complete, accurate information in order to make the best decisions for the organization.

So how does a robust portfolio management process impact project managers and project teams? Let us examine the power of strategically aligned projects.

Portfolio Management at the Project Level

As the portfolio management processes permeate the organization, project team members should begin to understand how their project aligns with organizational strategy. Project status reports feed directly into the categories of the strategic scorecard. Project managers are still responsible for project scope, quality, risk, cost, and schedule, as they have been traditionally. They now also partner with the business analyst to define how project results will align with strategic goals in the strategic plan and the business case.

For strategic projects, business analysts and project managers report directly to the executive project sponsor for ongoing direction and to the portfolio planning and management team for critical milestone control gate reviews. The filtering of information from the project manager up through the multi-layered functional chain of command is no longer required. Figures 2-4 and 2-5 depict these differences between the old hierarchical focus and the new strategic focus.

Figure 2-4—Old Hierarchical Focus

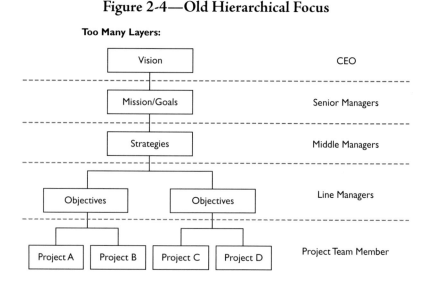

Too Many Layers:

Vision	CEO
Mission/Goals	Senior Managers
Strategies	Middle Managers
Objectives Objectives	Line Managers
Project A Project B Project C Project D	Project Team Member

Figure 2-5—New Strategic Focus

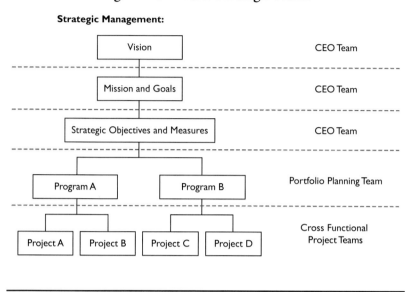

The executive project sponsor and the project team are accountable for business benefits. *Project profitability*—when project benefits exceed project and operational costs—is now the lowest unit of planning and control for the organization.

Under this new approach, cross-functional project teams become effective strategic tools employed by management to achieve goals. Consequently, management makes a considerable investment to build and sustain high-performing teams—small core project teams that are highly trained, multi-skilled, very experienced, and personally accountable. These core teams are *small but mighty*, co-located, and dedicated full-time to the project. This small, expert core team brings subject matter experts and subteams into the project at key points. The core team is empowered to make all project decisions. If the team encounters a barrier that is impeding forward progress, its project sponsor is just down the hall, available anytime, and committed to removing barriers in real time. Figures 2-6 and 2-7 depict the differences between the old and new project team structures.

Figure 2-6—Traditional Project Team Structure

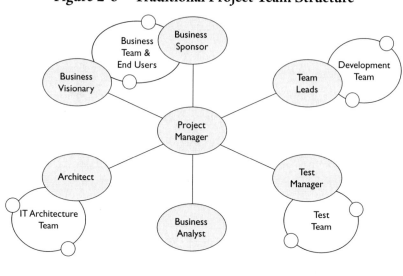

Figure 2-7—Core Project Team Structure

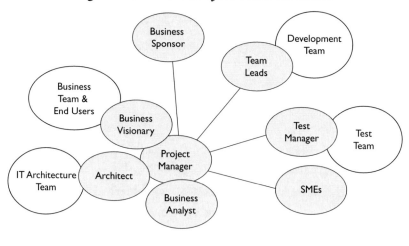

In addition to building and sustaining high-performing teams, management must be alert to environmental obstacles to project success. Often, management must simplify and streamline processes, eliminate outmoded policies, and remove barriers to team performance to create the optimal change-adaptive culture in which project teams can thrive.

The Role of the Program Management Office

Ideally, a program management office (PMO), or a similar center of excellence, facilitates the portfolio management process as a small, dedicated group serving under the direction of the executive team. The PMO is typically staffed by senior technologists, business analysts, and project managers. This staff is a proactive internal business/technology consulting group that provides subject matter expertise in all aspects of strategy execution and portfolio management. In this role, the PMO spends its time facilitating and providing decision-support information to the portfolio management team. The goal is to ensure that the organization is investing in the right project mix. PMO portfolio management support activities include:

- Developing and maintaining portfolio management processes and tools

- Aggregating metric data and strategic scorecard data

- Maintaining and reporting information in portfolio databases

- Mapping portfolios

- Preparing for and facilitating portfolio planning meetings

- Conducting feasibility, benchmark, and competitive studies

- Preparing business cases for proposed projects

- Measuring the value project outcomes bring to the organization

In addition, the PMO spends a considerable amount of time providing execution support to the project teams managing the highest priority projects. The goal is to build high-performing teams that execute flawlessly, leading to the earliest possible launch of the new product or service to achieve the greatest value to the organization. PMO project team support activities include:

- Facilitating project kickoff workshops

- Providing requirements elicitation and analysis support

- Coaching, mentoring, and team building

- Allocating resources

- Managing risk

- Preparing for control gate reviews

- Facilitating and assisting team leadership

- Formatting, compiling, and publishing reports

- Providing formal and informal training

Implementing an effective portfolio management process is no easy endeavor. It is essentially an organizational transformation initiative, significantly changing the way projects are conducted. The next section examines proven strategies for successfully implementing portfolio management.

Implementation Strategies

Implementing portfolio management processes involves an organization-wide change management effort, which is often led by the leadership team, supported by senior business analysts and project managers from the PMO. Simply training and supporting a single group of project managers and business analysts is of little help over the long term if the organization as a whole doesn't support the efforts and align them throughout. Likewise, it does not make sense to conduct rigorous strategic planning without a framework to link it to project teams and outcomes.

Implementing portfolio management is a significant endeavor requiring managers at all levels to change their way of selecting, investing in, and managing projects. The required cultural change can be painful and slow if the existing culture continues to determine the project selection methods. Implementing portfolio management requires success in several areas: soliciting executive support, taking inventory of and assessing the current projects in the portfolio, selecting and prioritizing new projects, and portfolio reporting.

Executive Support

Portfolio management implementation starts at the top and cascades down to all levels of the organization. To avoid false starts, the change initiative should be managed as a project. A formal portfolio management kickoff workshop brings together all key stakeholders, including the senior management team, functional managers who own project resources, senior project managers, business analysts, and other formal and informal leaders within the organization. The purpose of the workshop is to develop the charter and business case for implementing portfolio management and for establishing or expanding the role of the PMO.

Executive Seminars

Implementation should start at the top with an executive seminar that introduces the concepts and elements of strategic portfolio management. Such a seminar provides executives with awareness and education about where portfolio management fits in relation to other business management processes. The seminar should be designed to enable executives to arrive at consensus on moving forward to implement portfolio management. The seminar has several objectives, including introducing the idea of accompanying strategic planning with a strategic execution framework, enhancing leadership and management awareness of the importance of portfolio management, reviewing all components of effective strategy execution, and emphasizing the importance of a strategy-driven and adaptive culture.

Executive seminars held to discuss portfolio management strategies typically cover the importance of robust and dynamic strategic planning processes that include formulating strategic measures and themes. Portfolio planning and management must ensure that project initiatives align with greater organizational strategies. Executive seminars should also emphasize that program and project management can help ensure flawless project execution, highlighting the critical role of executive oversight through ongoing monitoring and control.

Assuming the executive team decides to move forward to implement portfolio management initiatives, the senior team leads the implementation and the PMO or a similar decision-support group facilitates implementation.

Portfolio Inventory and Assessment

After securing management's commitment to implement portfolio management, the PMO conducts a current-state analysis of active projects to determine which projects will be subjected to the portfolio management process. Serving as a resource to the portfolio management team, the PMO takes inventory of and organizes projects, making a first attempt at prioritizing them and preparing reports about the portfolio. The PMO also establishes a portfolio database to maintain an inventory of the projects in the portfolio, and implements a process to keep the information current.

The PMO first prioritizes projects by establishing boundaries to clearly define which projects will be subject to the portfolio management process. Corporate budgets usually allot only a limited amount of funding for department-specific initiatives managed within the business units, so the portfolio management team must spend its time managing only major strategic initiatives. The projects subjected to rigorous portfolio management may include those that meet one or more of the following criteria:

+ The project is cross-functional in nature

+ The project requires a significant investment of time and resources

+ The project is designed to achieve or advance one or more strategic goals

+ The project is high risk and/or involves new, unproven technology

When conducting an inventory and quick assessment of the current state of portfolio projects, the business analyst should prepare a portfolio summary report describing the project characteristics listed in Figure 2-8.

Project Selection

Portfolio planning and management teams follow a structured decision-making methodology when selecting the portfolio of valuable projects. Because not all project proposals can be funded, selecting projects requires the framework of a predetermined, structured, and defined decision-making process. The business analyst employs sophisticated business analysis techniques to gather and present to the portfolio management team the information that the team requires to make informed project selection decisions. The decision-support process is accompanied by supporting tools for assessing and prioritizing projects.

Many organizations support well over $100 million in project investments per year to improve performance. In addition to new-product development projects, organizations have a portfolio of in-

Figure 2-8—Portfolio Summary Report

Document	Information
Contact:	Executive in charge of the Enterprise Program Management Office
Purpose:	The purpose of this report is to provide real-time information on the status and priority of the portfolio of programs and projects across the enterprise.
Recipients:	Portfolio Planning and Management Team Program and Project Managers

Funded Active Programs and Projects

Priority Ranking	Project ID#	Project Name and Description	Project Sponsor	Project Manager	Project Objective	Business Benefits	Cost at Completion	Phase/Expected Completion Date	Date Last Reviewed

Unfunded Inactive Programs and Projects

Project ID#	Project Name and Description	Project Sponsor	Project Objective	Business Benefits	Cost at Completion	Project Manager	Phase/Expected Completion Date	Date of Last Evaluation	Priority Rating

ternal investments in IT, facilities, business process reengineering, new lines of business, corporate training, and cultural transformation initiatives. Portfolio management teams make the best investment decisions by focusing on three overarching project selection goals:

+ *Value maximization.* Maximize the value of the entire portfolio in traditional financial terms.

+ *Strategic alignment.* Break down project investments to ensure that they are appropriately tied to business strategies.

+ *Balance.* Achieve the appropriate balance of projects in the portfolio.

Balance is perhaps the most difficult goal to achieve because portfolios are balanced according to different areas of business value. For example, a portfolio can be balanced by its types of projects (e.g., research and development, IT, new-product development, product-line enhancements), by the duration of its projects (e.g., long term, short term), by the risk level of its projects (e.g., high risk, "sure wins"), and by the number of its retooling projects (i.e., technology and/or business process improvement projects needed to remain competitive).

Project Prioritization

Once the projects that are worth including in the portfolio management process are chosen, that group of projects—the narrowed portfolio—must be prioritized. This step includes determining prioritization criteria based on strategic plans, goals, and performance measures. Typical prioritization criteria include organizational factors, cost/benefit analysis, customer satisfaction, stakeholder relations, risk analysis, technical uncertainty, and cultural change impact. If the organization does not have a mature strategic planning process, this step might be difficult. In such a case, it may be necessary to hold to a strategic planning session to determine key strategic goals and measures.

Decision-support tools and reports are designed to support portfolio assessments according to their business value.[10] It is imperative that organizations use a project prioritization tool to assist in making project investment decisions. A senior business analyst from within the PMO develops and pilots a prototype project prioritization tool to ensure that the projects appear to be prioritized appropriately. The business analyst then adjusts the prioritization tool on the basis of the pilot results, and presents the prioritized list of projects and the project prioritization tool to the portfolio planning and management team for approval. Figure 2-9 offers a sample project ranking tool.

Portfolio Reporting

The PMO prepares an initial set of portfolio reports for presentation to the portfolio planning and management team. Elements in the reports typically include a list of projects ranked by priority, including summary information about each project obtained during the quick assessment; a status report for each project; and portfolio mapping reports. The PMO determines which kind of information will mean the most to the portfolio management team, and should continue to refine and improve that information as much as possible before delivering the report. Remember a golden rule: keep it simple.

Portfolio reports and graphical maps are essential to make the entire portfolio of projects visible for executive assessment. Portfolio maps are effective tools to visually demonstrate the link between projects and strategic goals. Projects are designed to reach strategic goals, but the business analyst has to define that connection. In addition, portfolio maps are created to chart projects to strategic report categories, to risk levels, and according to financial return (e.g., net present value—cash value over a period of time, economic value added—how project deliverables affect earnings). Senior business

Figure 2-9—Sample Project Ranking Tool

Solution Option Selection Criteria	Weight (W)	Initial Rating [R]	Final Rating [W * R]
Customer Satisfaction 1--10 Low High			
Strategic Alignment 1--10 Low High			
Employee Satisfaction 1--10 Low High			
Increased Revenue 1--10 Low High			
Reduced Cost 1--10 Low High			
Longevity 1--10 Short – Long – Use for 2 Yrs Use 4+ Yrs			
Size of Investment 10--1 Small—$25–100K Large— >$100K 6 Months 12 Months			
Project Complexity Risk 10--1 Relatively Simple Relatively Complex Straightforward Poorly Understood			
New Technology Risk 10--1 Proven S/W H/W Unproven S/W H/W			
Benefit Risk 10--1 Known Committed Risky Benefits Out-Year Estimates			
TOTAL RATING			

Legend:

1. *Customer Satisfaction*: impact of project on external customers
2. *Business Results*: impact of project on strategic goals
3. *Employee Satisfaction*: impact of project on employee retention
4. *Revenue*: impact of project on increased revenue
5. *Cost*: low versus high cost to fund the project
6. *Longevity*: length of time the enterprise will benefit from the new product or service
7. *Size of Investment*: large versus small investment risk
8. *Project Complexity Risk*: simple versus complex project
9. *New Technology Risk*: proven technology versus cutting edge/unproven
10. *Benefit Risk*: risk to realizing projected benefits

analysts should place sufficient focus on procedural and cultural issues, keeping the process simple and straightforward to demonstrate the business value of disciplined portfolio management. Figures 2-10, 2-11, and 2-12 offer sample portfolio mapping reports.

Implementing portfolio management is an arduous task. Many organizations have been unable to establish and maintain an effective practice to manage their project investments. Soliciting executive support, portfolio inventory and assessment, project selection, project prioritization, and portfolio reporting are all essential to success.

Challenges

Even well-established portfolio management systems encounter challenges. Difficulties include:

• Too many off-strategy projects, disconnects between spending breakdowns and priorities

Figure 2-10—Portfolio Mapping Report – Market Attractiveness versus Ease of Implementation

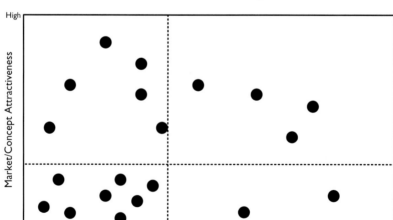

Figure 2-11—Portfolio Mapping Report – Product Mix

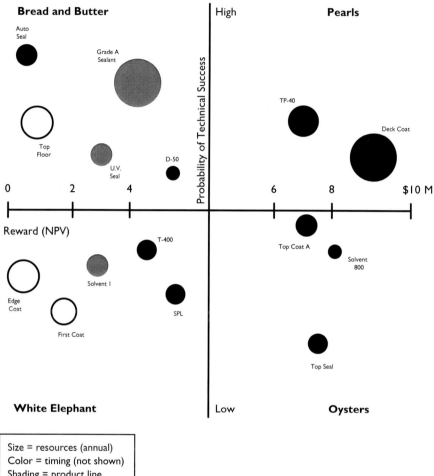

- Too many unfit, weak, mediocre projects; inadequate success rates at product launch

- Weak go/no-go decisions, projects tend to take on a life of their own, poorly performing projects are not terminated

- Project density is too great, far too many projects for limited resources, cycle times and success rates suffer

Figure 2-12—Portfolio Mapping Report – Probability of Success versus Net Present Value

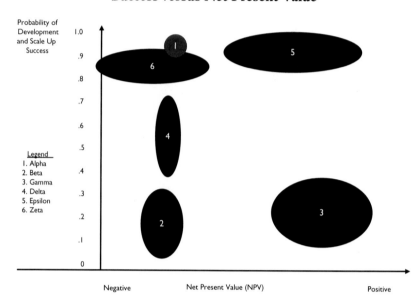

- ✦ Inadequate resource planning and allocation processes, over-allocated project team members

- ✦ Too many trivial projects in the new-product pipeline (e.g., modifications, updates, enhancements)

- ✦ Not enough major-breakthrough, competitive-advantage projects, probably a result of reduced cycle time with insufficient resources

- ✦ Inability to measure investment metrics

As they help design and implement project portfolio management processes for their organizations, business analysts should pay special attention to these challenges and work to avoid or mitigate their impact. Using the best practices presented in the following section can help.

Best Practices

The following portfolio management best practices can go a long way toward preventing typical challenges. Failing to understand and follow these guidelines may compromise the overall portfolio management implementation process.

Strategic enterprise-wide focus—specific and measurable strategic goals as a foundation for selecting projects. After establishing strategic goals, themes, and measures, the business analyst should filter all major change initiatives through the portfolio management process to receive funding.

Simplicity—simple, straightforward portfolio management processes. Keeping portfolio management processes simple can facilitate their acceptance on an organizational level. Most executives have an aversion to complex processes and bureaucratic paperwork. The business analyst and the PMO can further assuage executive resistance by doing most of the work.

Early filtering criteria—basic requirements or watershed criteria. A project must fulfill basic requirements to be considered strategic and to become a candidate for selection and funding. For example, it's important to confirm that the project delivers a cross-functional benefit. Other common filters include alignment with the organizational mission, business threshold minimums (e.g., ROI, cost/ benefit ratio), and compliance with organizational constraints (e.g., current technology).

Standards—standard templates for the business case and project proposal. Use standard templates to ensure that decision-makers always review consistent information from project to project. This is essential to make defensible judgments on the project's priority. See Appendix A for a sample business case template.

Project ranking tool—standard project assessment, selection, and prioritization tools. The project ranking decision-support tool usually contains ranking criteria that are based on strategic goals. Assign relative weights to each criterion, determine a project's ranking based on the criteria, and calculate a score (or priority rating) for each project. See Figure 2-9 for a sample project ranking tool.

Portfolio reviews—regular portfolio review meetings to ensure balance and strategic consistency among projects. Conduct portfolio review meetings to assess the entire portfolio for balance and strategic alignment, and to review new project proposals and ongoing project status at key checkpoints for go/no-go decisions.

Process support—support for the process in terms of process, tools, information and facilitation. A PMO, business analysis center of excellence, or a similar support group helps define and continuously improve portfolio management processes, maintain portfolio records, and prepare accurate decision-support information for the portfolio management team.

Investment analysis measures—measurement of the portfolio's value to determine the return on project investments. Well-defined portfolios, audited results, and post-project benefit analyses are key to understanding the actual value of portfolio investments and management practices.

These best practices are essential for success. Organizations lacking in sophisticated business analysis practices are at risk. As IT governance becomes an adopted practice, robust portfolio management practices are indispensable management tools.

Part II builds on the portfolio management methods described in this chapter, and delves deeper into more advanced portfolio management techniques organizations may use depending on the maturity of their portfolio management and business analysis practices.

Endnotes

1. David P. Norton. "Project Balanced Scorecards—A Tool for Alignment, Teamwork and Results," *ProjectWorld & The World Congress for Business Analysts Conference Proceedings*, November 17, 2005. Orlando, FL.

2. Ibid.

3. Ibid.

4. Kathleen B. Hass. *Professionalizing Business Analysis: Breaking the Cycle of Challenged Projects*, 2008. Vienna, VA: Management Concepts.

5. Eugene Lukac. "Avoiding Worst Practices in IT Spending," *CSC World*, September-November 2004. Online at www.csc.com/aboutus/cscworld/sept_nov_04/articles/avoiding_worst_practices_septnov04.pdf (accessed March 7, 2006).

6. Ibid.

7. Stephanie Overby. "Backsourcing Pain," *CIO Magazine*, October 11, 2005. Online at http://www.cio.com.au/index.php/id;1796120911;fp;16;fpid;0 (accessed August 15, 2007).

8. Center for Business Practices. *Project Portfolio Management Maturity: A Benchmark of Current Business Practices*. Havertown, PA: Center for Business Practices, June 2005. Online at http://whitepapers.zdnet.com/whitepaper.aspx?&compid=9785&docid=158347 (accessed September 19, 2007).

9. Federal CIO Council. *A Summary of First Practices and Lessons Learned in Information Technology Portfolio Management*, March 2002. Online at http://www.cio.gov/documents/BPC_portfolio_final.pdf (accessed August 18, 2007).

10. R.G. Cooper, S.J. Edgett, and E.J. Lleinschmidt, "Portfolio Management in New Product Development: Lessons from the Leaders, Phase I," *Project Portfolio Management, Selecting and Prioritizing Projects for Competitive Advantage*, James S. Pennypacker and Lowell D. Dye, editors, 1999. Havertown, PA: Center for Business Practices.

Part II

Using Portfolio Management to Achieve Strategic Goals

*P*art II builds on the basic strategic planning and portfolio management processes outlined in Part I with a more in-depth discussion of advanced portfolio management processes used by successful organizations today.

Chapter 3 introduces the enterprise architecture—the infrastructural design and connections among an organization's systems—and describes how architectural work captures and portrays business and technical information in an interconnected way that promotes consistency between business operations and their enabling IT products and services. Chapter 3 also focuses on the subcomponent business architecture, which the business analyst creates and maintains to guide the execution of organizational strategy through managed change.

Strategic planning and the creation of a business architecture provide a firm foundation for understanding where an organization is today and where it wants to be in the future. From this foundation, organizations must select the best initiatives to manage the changes necessary to reach goals as quickly as possible, and with the least cost and risk. Chapter 4 describes the business analyst's role in incorporating feasibility studies into the portfolio management process, making project selection more effective.

Supporting information from the feasibility studies and the business architecture is combined with a formal business case to present a complete decision package to the portfolio management team. Chapter 5 outlines the business case in detail, and then discusses the business analyst's role in developing the decision package, which additionally includes scoping and defining business opportunities and conducting initial risk assessments.

Chapter 6 describes how the business analyst acts on the information collected and analyzed during the pre-project portfolio selection activities by managing project value and measuring business benefits after deploying the project solution.

Chapter 3

The Value of the Business Architecture in Strategy Execution

In This Chapter:

- Defining the Enterprise Architecture

- Defining the Business Architecture

- Business Architects

- Architecture Frameworks

- Creating the Business Architecture

- Challenges

- Best Practices

In today's world of global competition and mergers and acquisitions, organizations are large, complex, and often in some state of chaos. Business processes and IT systems have been built from the ground up as businesses rapidly changed and evolved. As business entities have increased in complexity, they have begun to employ engineering principles to assist in managing organizational complexity and change. Engineering disciplines have historically used blueprints and architectural drawings to design and construct complex systems. To bring order to the rather chaotic business environment and to ensure that costly IT infrastructure supports the business, developing an *enterprise architecture* to make the components of the enterprise visible is becoming a widespread practice.

An essential element of the enterprise architecture is the *business architecture*, which is created and maintained by the business analyst. The business architecture provides a unified structure that guides the *execution of strategy through managed change*. This chapter first defines the overarching enterprise architecture, and then delves more specifically into the business sub-architecture.

Defining the Enterprise Architecture

Implementing business strategy and solving business problems are the drivers of major business change initiatives. Comparing the current and future states of the enterprise provides a common understanding of changes that the business must make to achieve its goals. As the business changes, rich pictures and textual statements embodied in the enterprise architecture makes the organization visible and enables business units and supporting IT systems to align. Architectural work captures and portrays business and technical information in an interconnected way that promotes consistency between business operations and their enabling IT products and services.

Enterprise architecture is all about understanding the complexity of the business by decomposing and documenting its components. It is widely viewed as a comprehensive framework used to align all components of an organization to its overall strategy.

Industry experts provide various definitions of enterprise architecture. The Open Group, a business and technology consortium bringing together best practices from across the industry, defines an enterprise as:[1]

> *Any collection of organizations that has a common set of goals and/or a single bottom line. In that sense, an enterprise can be a government agency, a whole corporation, a division of a corpo-*

ration, a single department, or a chain of geographically distant organizations linked together by common ownership.

The term enterprise *in the context of* enterprise architecture *can be used to denote both an entire enterprise, encompassing all of its information systems, and a specific domain within the enterprise. In both cases, the architecture crosses multiple systems, and multiple functional groups within the enterprise.*

The Institute of Electrical and Electronics Engineers (IEEE) is an organization composed of engineers, scientists, and students that is best known for developing standards for computers and the electronics industry. The IEEE Standard 1471-2000 defines architecture as "the fundamental organization of a system, embodied in its components, their relationships to each other and the environment, and the principles governing its design and evolution."[2]

The Open Group contends that architecture has two meanings. One definition suggests that architecture is "a formal description of a system, or a detailed plan of the system at component level to guide its implementation." Another definition calls architecture the "structure of components, their inter-relationship, and the principles and guidelines governing their design and evolution over time."[3]

Using an enterprise architecture to address persistent disappointment in IT investments has become a significant practice within private industries and the U.S. federal government. The Open Group goes on to note the use of enterprise architecture to support IT as a key factor to business success:[4]

- ⁺ The enterprise architecture supports the business by providing technology and process structure for an IT strategy, thus making IT a strong and flexible asset that is indispensable to achieving competitive advantage.

- ⁺ The enterprise architecture provides a strategic context for the evolution of IT.

◆ The enterprise architecture enables an organization to achieve the right balance between IT efficiency and business innovation.

Dennis A. Stevenson discusses the value of enterprise architecture in a paper he presented to the Department of Information Systems at the University of Cape Town in June 1995:[5]

> In a large modern enterprise, a rigorously defined framework is necessary to be able to capture a vision of the "entire system" in all its dimensions and complexity. Enterprise architecture (EA) is a framework which is able to coordinate the many facets that make up the fundamental essence of an enterprise. It is the master plan which "acts as an integrating force" between aspects of business planning such as goals, visions, strategies, and governance principles; aspects of business operations such as business terms, organization structures, processes, and data; aspects of automation such as application systems and databases; and the enabling technological infrastructure of the business such as computers, operating systems, and networks.

A complete enterprise architecture encompasses both technical and business-related architectural components. A typical enterprise architecture consists of five sub-architectures: business, information, application, technology, and security. The following section discusses, in detail, the business sub-architecture, which is the business analyst's responsibility.

Defining the Business Architecture

The *business architecture* serves as the overarching business model, constructed to provide a view of the business so that the other four architectures can then be designed in alignment. Also referred to as the *enterprise business architecture*, or the *business area architecture* (if its scope is one business unit within the enterprise), it defines the value streams, or processes, that flow value from the organization to its customers. The business architecture also defines the relationship of all external entities, as well as what the organization must produce to satisfy its customers and compete in the marketplace.

A website highlighting *Enterprise Business Architecture: The Formal Link between Strategy and Results*, written by Ralph Whittle and Conrad B. Myrick, notes:[6]

> The Enterprise Business Architecture defines the formal link between the enterprise business strategy and the results predicted from supporting strategic initiatives. The EBA provides a single source and comprehensive repository of knowledge from which corporate initiatives will evolve and link. The evolution occurs from a fully integrated enterprise model of the business to all IT, organizational, and security architectures. The EBA also provides integration capabilities for software development, packaged software configuration, and process improvement initiatives.
>
> By using the EBA, enterprises can formally engineer solutions that directly link to the desired results defined by the enterprise strategy. These are not "seat of the pants" type business projects, but rather "business by design."

The business architecture fosters a common business and technology planning structure. It records both a current view of the business and the desired future state. The current view facilitates the management of day-to-day business operations and supports continuous improvement efforts. The future or strategic view is designed to facilitate planning for broad, radical transformation initiatives. As new business opportunities turn into proposed new projects, the enterprise architecture views are used to determine the impact of change on the business and on the IT systems supporting the business.

The business architecture helps to ensure the integration of the policies, processes, and IT systems as they change by:

+ Documenting the current state of the business

- Developing the future state of the business to bring the strategic vision into view

- Analyzing the gaps between the current and future states to determine the extent of change required to achieve the vision

- Providing a context in which to assess proposed new projects

- Helping identify which new business opportunities to pursue

Components

The *business architecture* consists of a set of documents, models, workflows, events, and diagrams organized to present information about the business in terms that members of the business and technical communities can understand. Components of the business architecture may vary, but they typically include descriptive documentation for the business vision, mission, strategy, functions, rules, policies, procedures, processes, organizations, competencies, and locations that together constitute the business as a system for delivery of value. The business architecture is essentially "a blueprint of how an organization's business systems should interoperate in the fulfillment of the mission and business objectives of the organization."[7]

Scope

The scope of the business architecture development effort depends on the availability of resources, the time allocated to complete architecture work, and the needs, complexity, and maturity of the enterprise. In small, easily understood organizations, the business architecture likely consists of a simple set of organization charts, business plans, policies, and procedures. In large, complex organizations, the business architecture might consist of the traditional documents and charts that describe the business mission, organizational structure, and policies, accompanied by abstract representations of the more complex components of the business. These representations take the form of models, graphs, matrices, and structured text, and they are used to depict the complex interrelationship between various components of the enterprise.

Whatever form the architectural views take, most business architecture efforts have a common goal: to bring order to the complexity of businesses today. Because businesses are undergoing massive amounts of change, the business architecture is becoming a powerful change management tool. The business architecture must not only provide structure and efficiency, but also remain flexible enough to accommodate different business strategies, functions, rules, and components—all of which seem to change constantly. The business architecture focuses on the functional aspects of the business from a number of perspectives:[8]

- *People*—the human resources of the business and their knowledge, skills, roles, responsibilities, and capabilities

- *Process*—the external and internal processes used by the business to flow value through the organization to the customers and, ultimately, to achieve its goals

- *Functions*—the functions required to support the processes

- *Data and information*—the data and information required to flow through the processes

Tools and Techniques

Determining how to develop the business architecture involves reviewing available tools to support the development, storage, presentation, and enhancement of architecture components. As with architecture methodologies and frameworks, enterprise architecture tools to support the architectural development process are still emerging. Whether common desktop tools or powerful modeling and management tools are used, it is important to standardize and consolidate the collection of architectural drawings and documents into a single repository to support enterprise analysis. Numerous techniques are available to help architects model, store, manage, and share information about the enterprise. We present just a few.

Business Scenarios

Business scenarios are perhaps the single most important technique that can be used to develop the business architecture. Business scenarios help the architecture team identify and understand the true business needs. They can be used to depict what should happen when planned and unplanned events occur, and to help understand the magnitude of necessary changes to business processes.

Business scenarios can describe a business process or business problem; the business and technology environment; the business objective; the human resources (called actors) that execute the scenario and their place in the business model; the roles, responsibilities, and measures of success; computer actors; and the desired outcome of the scenario.[9]

Models

In addition, a variety of modeling techniques are often used to accompany the business scenarios. Models are used to capture business and technology elements in graphical form to help others comprehend business scenarios and to facilitate the validation of business scenarios.[10] The following modeling techniques represent just a few of those commonly used during the development of a business architecture. Refer to another volume in this series, *Getting It Right: Business Requirements Analysis Tools and Techniques*, for more detailed information about models commonly used in business analysis.

+ *Reference model*—a structure that enables system modules and interfaces to be described in a consistent manner

+ *Business process model*—a network of activities that consistently and routinely produces a planned result

+ *Use case model*—a model that can describe either business processes or systems functions, depending on the focus of the modeling effort

+ *Class model*—a model that describes static information and relationships between information and informational behaviors

Bringing about large-scale business change requires attention to both the organizational and technological aspects of change. All too often, projects involving significant IT components have difficulty resolving issues involving organizational structure, processes, and people, which causes costly delays in getting the new business solution up and running and places the expected business benefits at risk. Building and maintaining the enterprise architecture ensures that significant change initiatives will focus on all potential areas of change.

Business Architects

As the business analysis practice matures, a small group of *business architects*, also know as *architecture analysts,* is emerging. Business architects are typically senior business analysts who focus—sometimes exclusively—on documenting the current and future states of the business so that everyone has a correct, accurate, and consistent view of where the business is (the "as is" state) and where it is going (the "to be" state). These business architects may also keep an eye on the work done by project analysts to ensure they are adhering to the standards set forth in the business architecture. If necessary, business architects may extract architectural components from projects that will change the business architecture. In addition, business architects closely monitor changes to the business vision, strategy, and goals to ensure the future state business architecture accurately represents the future vision.

Meta Group, a provider of information technology research, advisory services, and strategic consulting, predicts that by 2008, 40 percent of enterprise architects will have primary expertise in business strategy or process engineering and may no longer reside under the IT umbrella. This reflects the rising importance of business architecture and the need for a more balanced skillset (beyond technical architecture). Scott Bittler, a vice president at Gartner Research who specializes in enterprise architecture, IT strategy, and portfolio management, contends that:[11]

> As the discipline of enterprise architecture has broadened beyond technical architecture in recent years to include business, information, and solution architecture, deep technical expertise is even less essential—and can be a liability if the individual has a "favorite" vendor/product.

According to Bittler, effective business architects have key characteristics; business architects are:[12]

+ *Enthusiastic*—they have a passion about their work.

+ *Technology-agnostic*—they are vendor/product-neutral and maintain an objective perspective.

+ *Broadly knowledgeable about technology*—it is important that an architect understand enough about the broad range of technologies to be able to engage in discussions with technical experts.

+ *Well-respected and influential*—architects need the support of senior IT and business managers, and they need the ability to influence those managers and the IT organization at large.

+ *Able to represent a constituency*—members of an business architecture team have a constituency—the part of the organization they represent in the process.

+ *Articulate and persuasive*—business architects must spend substantial time communicating and educating. Therefore, it is important that they have the skills to clearly communicate ideas in a persuasive, compelling manner.

+ *Persistent*—business architects are strategically inspired change agents. People tend to resist change, and this is certainly true when changes are instituted by architecture-related efforts. Therefore, it is critical to be persistent in pursuit of positive transformation.

+ *Good at "helicoptering"*—business architects have the rare ability to "zoom out" to discuss business strategy with the CEO and a minute later, "zoom in" to discuss complex details with a technical expert without getting lost.

+ *Strategic*—architects must be strategically driven, but they should also balance strategy with effective, tactical operations. Strategic ideas contribute to defining or fulfilling the transformations described in the business strategy of the organization, while tactical operations execute those ideas.

+ *Focused on what is truly best for the organization*—limited personal agendas.

+ *Knowledgeable about the business*—business architects are leaders, and therefore they must have a strong interest in and understanding of the business and its strategic direction, dysfunctions, and strengths.

+ *Able to facilitate*—business architects frequently facilitate content development meetings or lead subcommittees, which makes effective group facilitation skills important.

+ *Able to negotiate*—it is important to seek the win-win positions/solutions on issues when developing architecture content. Effective negotiation skills are invaluable for resolving contentious situations.

+ *Focused on the long term*: The idea is to take a series of short-term steps that not only deliver immediate value but also contribute toward achieving a long-term vision for the enterprise. Focus on identifying and driving toward that long-term goal.

+ *Able to lead*—architects should take the initiative to persuade, inspire, motivate, and influence others. They should also focus on attaining a high level of stakeholder buy-in for important decisions.

This list doesn't include a strong understanding of enterprise architecture as a key characteristic of business architects per se, because those who possess all or most of these traits can learn architecture best practices quickly and can rapidly become effective architects.

Architecture Frameworks

Because the business architecture is a sub-component of the larger enterprise architecture, it is prudent to use common frameworks, tools, and techniques to develop the subsets of the enterprise architecture. Engineering architectural approaches are emerging as a useful method for capturing complex knowledge about organizations and technology. Enterprise architectural approaches range from broad, enterprise-focused approaches to scaled-down efforts aimed at specific domains.

Not every business requires a comprehensive business architecture, and those that do may not require all possible views or representations of the business.[13] Therefore, it is important to determine the specific requirements that are driving the business architecture effort, who intends to use the resulting architecture, and how. It's important to understand the expectations of both the business and the IT groups.

Once user requirements are fully understood, documented, and approved, the business architect determines which architectural framework and corresponding tools and techniques to use to create the architecture. Three common architecture frameworks include the Open Group Architecture Framework, the Zachman Framework for Enterprise Architecture, and the POLDAT Framework for Business Process Reengineering. Each framework is different and has associated pros and cons.

The Open Group Architecture Framework

The Open Group Architecture Framework (TOGAF™) is a valuable resource for businesses embarking upon the development of an enterprise architecture.[14] It consists of three elements: the *TOGAF™ Architecture Development Method* (ADM)—a description of the processes and techniques needed to develop an enterprise architecture; the *Enterprise Continuum*—a virtual repository of architectural assets from which to choose; the *TOGAF™ Resource Base*—a set of guidelines, templates, and other reference information to help architecture analysts use the ADM.

For the organization that is new to enterprise architecture, the TOGAF™ set of tools, templates, and guidelines provides an invaluable place to start. TOGAF™ resources are available for free and may be used by any organization wishing to develop an enterprise architecture for internal use.

The Zachman Framework for Enterprise Architecture

Organizations typically use a defined framework that provides a common classification scheme for descriptive representations of an enterprise. One such framework that both public and private organizations have adopted is the *Zachman Framework for Enterprise Architecture*. Indeed, the United States Federal Chief Information Officers Council has adopted this framework as part of the Federal Enterprise Architecture Framework Standard.[15] The purpose of the Zachman Framework is described below:[16]

> *The Zachman Framework is a comprehensive classification scheme for descriptive representations (models) of an enterprise. First conceptualized nearly two decades ago by John Zachman, it has evolved to become a universal schematic for defining and describing today's complex enterprise systems and for managing the multiple perspectives of an organization's information and knowledge infrastructure.*

The framework has become widely employed because it provides a comprehensive view of business domains and their information characteristics. The value of this framework is in its integration of key elements; it provides a common language and a structure for describing a business entity. "Integration does not happen by accident," says John Zachman. Without a unifying framework, an organization may be a disintegrated, poorly functioning enterprise, fraught with redundancies, inefficiencies, and interoperability issues. The Zachman Framework (Figure 3-1) is complex and comprehensive.[17] It is presented in a matrix format where the columns represent the interrogatives, or the questions that must be answered to build a business component as part of the architecture (e.g., what, how, where, who, when, why). The rows describe the perspectives of managers of the enterprise: scope, business model, system model, technology model, and detailed representations.

Figure 3-1—The Zachman Framework

Copyright © 1987 John A. Zachman. Reprinted with permission.

The POLDAT Framework

An alternative, simpler structure that is often used in business process reengineering projects is the POLDAT Framework for Business Process Reengineering, referred to as the *hexagon of change* or the *six domains of change*.[18] This framework provides an easily understood approach to defining the scope of business transformation initiatives. The model develops artifacts (e.g., documents, tables, matrices, graphs, models) and organizes them into the following domains:

- *Process*—the business processes that flow value from the organization to the customer. What are our current processes, and do we have opportunities to improve those processes? What is the desired state of business operations?

- *Organization*—the organizational entities that operate the business processes, including the management teams, staff positions, roles, competencies, knowledge, and skills. What changes in culture, capabilities, competencies, teams, organizations, and training are needed to accomplish the necessary business change? What support systems are needed to accept the new business solution and ensure it operates efficiently?

- *Location*—the location of the business units and other organizational entities, such as call centers and distribution centers. What effects will the change have on geography, people, infrastructure, data, and applications? What physical facilities are needed to deploy the change?

- *Data*—the data and information that are the currency of the organization, flowing through the processes to accomplish the business functions. What new information content and structures are needed to meet the strategies? What data security is needed?

+ *Applications*—the IT applications that enable the business processes to operate efficiently and provide decision-support information to the management team. Which applications should be changed and/or developed? How will the applications be integrated?

+ *Technology*—the enabling technology that supports the operation of the processes and applications. What hardware, system software, and communications networks are needed to support the business? How can we leverage existing and emerging technology?

In the early stages of an architecture effort for a major project, each domain listed above is defined as either in scope or out of scope. In this framework, artifacts in the process, organization, and location categories constitute elements of the business architecture. When they are accompanied by artifacts in the data, applications, and technology categories, the entire enterprise architecture is complete.

The value of this framework lies in its simplicity. Organizations embarking on the first iteration of their enterprise architecture would do well to first use the POLDAT framework and then move on to a more comprehensive approach if appropriate.

Creating the Business Architecture

One approach to building a business architecture involves the following steps:

1. Build a core architecture team

2. Determine the sponsor, business drivers, and scope for the business architecture effort

3. Plan the business architecture activities

4. Create the architectural components

5. Conduct a quality review and baseline the business architecture

This is not a mandatory process for creating and maintaining the business architecture. The process steps and the sequence of activities may vary considerably depending on the drivers of the architecture effort. For example, some enterprises begin by collecting all descriptive information relevant to the current state of the business, identifying gaps, and developing documents, lists, or graphics to fill in the gaps. Others begin by developing the architecture for the desired future state of the enterprise.

Build a Core Architecture Team

As the business architect embarks upon the effort to create and maintain the business architecture, it is wise to first build a core team of subject matter experts (SMEs) to ensure that the models and documents represent the collective wisdom about the organization from various business and technical perspectives. We recommend the following experts:

- *Project manager*—involve an experienced project manager to help develop the project scope and prepare time and cost estimates.

- *Business visionaries*—involve business SMEs from all areas of the organization that are affected by the effort. Recruit creative thinkers—futurists, if possible.

- *Business architect*—involve an experienced architect to provide oversight and advice during the effort.

- *Technology architect*—involve an experienced IT architect to ensure alignment between the business and technical architectures.

Collaborating with these professionals to plan, create, refine, and determine the business architecture structure can greatly smooth the progress of the architecture project. This team can estimate costs and resource requirements, identify key stakeholders, get the right people involved in architectural activities, facilitate business architecture design, development and review meetings, and negotiate decisions.

Determine the Sponsor, Business Drivers, and Scope of the Business Architecture Effort

The business analyst should develop a description of the business entities the architecture is focusing on to create a high-level understanding of the current state of the business and to begin understanding the scope of the effort.

The business analyst should collect and review all existing documentation about the business entity under consideration. The scope and level of detail needed for the current-state description depend on the business drivers for the creation of the architecture, and on whether current architectural descriptions already exist. At this point, the goal is to create a matrix of architectural assets that will meet the immediate business need and identify which business architecture models and documents, also known as *building blocks,* already exist and which need to be updated or created.

The business analyst should prepare a list of the key stakeholders of the initiative and conduct a stakeholder analysis. Enlist the help of a sponsor and define their expectations for the business architecture effort. Review the list of architectural assets with key stakeholders and the sponsor to gain consensus on the scope of the effort. Include stakeholders that will use the architectural models and documents (e.g., business analysts, project managers, IT architects and developers, business representatives) to ensure they are complete and fit for use.

Plan the Business Architecture Activities

Once the sponsor, key stakeholders, and scope of the architectural effort are understood, enlist the assistance of a senior project manager and an experienced architect to help plan architecture activities. It's possible to manage the creation of the business architecture as a standalone project, or to manage those activities as part of a larger project. Follow these steps to plan the architectural effort:

+ Select what is referred to as *relevant business architectural viewpoints*—lines of business or business units (e.g., operations, management, financial, engineering). These viewpoints must be in the project's scope so the architect can document the organization's key capabilities.

+ Determine the appropriate framework and approach to building the architectural assets.

+ Identify appropriate tools and techniques to use to capture, model, and analyze architectural models and documents. Depending on the degree of sophistication warranted, these may include simple documents and spreadsheets or more sophisticated architectural tools.

+ Determine which architectural assets or components (e.g., documents, graphics, matrices, drawings) to create or update. Limit the set of assets that will be produced to reduce the risk of "analysis paralysis." Not all artifacts are produced for every effort.

+ Determine how to store the artifacts. This may involve creating a repository to serve as the archiving mechanism.

As plans emerge, a number of considerations must be taken into account. The plans in place must meet the business need. Ensure that the approach will support business planning activities and help determine the scope of change initiatives. This decision will help determine the level of detail needed when building the architecture.

Comply with—or develop, if nonexistent—organizational standards for each of the architecture's deliverables. Developing architectural standards can be a difficult and time-consuming task. It's also necessary to decide whether to build the architecture using a top-down holistic approach or a bottom-up, change-initiative-driven approach that creates only a limited set of architectural models and documents to satisfy a particular project's needs. Limit the size and complexity of the architectural effort by creating or maintaining only the components necessary to meet the needs of the business drivers. In addition, decide whether to build only the future state (to-be) model, the current state (as-is) model, or both. This could depend in part by how much documentation on the current state already exists.

Create the Architectural Components

Once the plan has been drafted and approved, and funding is available, the architecture team then creates the documents and models that describe the core organizational components. As noted, these may include some or all the following elements of the business model: vision, mission, strategy, goals, themes, objectives measures, rules, processes, features, functions, organizational structures, roles, locations, competencies, data requirements, business and operational plans, annual reports, and the like. Once again, create only the artifacts that are required to meet the specific business need to avoid investing too heavily in building the business architecture.

Review the architectural components to ensure they are complete. It is helpful to build a requirements traceability matrix to ensure that architectural components meet the business need and to validate that all requirements within the scope of the architecture effort have been addressed.

After creating the set of architectural components, identify those that are likely to be reused by other projects (e.g., working practices, roles, business rules, business relationships, job descriptions) and publish them for the appropriate stakeholders. Archive all architectural components in the architecture repository. Prepare the final architecture report documenting the rationale for structure and composition, and other decisions (e.g., whether to build or not to build certain elements of the architecture).

Conduct a Quality Review and Baseline the Business Architecture

A baseline establishes a starting point or condition for future changes. Review the architecture artifacts, ensuring the requirements for this effort have been met. In addition, validate each artifact to determine not only that it is fit for use to fulfill the immediate need, but also to support subsequent work in the other architecture domains, and to ensure compliance with organizational standards. At the conclusion of the review, refine the business architecture as necessary to close any gaps uncovered during these final quality reviews. As a final step, review and refine business performance measures, ensuring performance metrics are defined for all elements of the strategic scorecard.

Challenges

Introducing an enterprise architecture as a means to overcome the alignment deficits between business and IT units is an arduous task. It involves resolving differences in interests, perceptions, and goals. Business architects must overcome some unique challenges to successfully develop the business architecture:

- If the organization is not mature enough to develop a business architecture, there may not be enough funds or resources for the effort. The business architect should attempt to involve stakeholders, offering a considerable amount of education about business architectures if necessary, and employing sophisticated influence strategies to enlist adequate support for the effort.

- The IT organization may believe that it owns the business architecture because it has the modeling skills, thus preventing proper business ownership. This may result in a business architecture that does not truly represent the current or future state of the organization from a business perspective.

- Strategic plans, strategic goals, and/or the current-state business documentation don't capture the future strategic direction in enough depth to create the future-state architecture.

- There are no senior business analysts that have the knowledge and skills to create and maintain the business architecture.

Best Practices

What makes a successful business architecture endeavor? Lessons learned during previous architectural effort offer insight. The following success factors may come into play, depending on the culture and maturity of the organization:

- Using a standard framework (e.g., POLDAT) and tool set

- Requiring standard business architecture deliverables for all major change initiatives

- Requiring skilled architects to report to a central group (e.g., PMO, center of excellence)

- Focusing on the approach that will bring the most value to the enterprise

- ◆ Performing tradeoff analysis to resolve any conflicts among the different views

- ◆ Validating that the business architecture initiative supports overall strategic goals, organizational principles, and short-term objectives and constraints.

Endnotes

1. The Open Group. *The Open Group Architecture Framework, Frequently Asked Questions.* Online at http://www.opengroup.org/architecture/togaf8-doc/arch/toc.html (accessed September 5, 2007).

2. Institute of Electrical and Electronics Engineers. *IEEE Recommended Practice For Architectural Description Of Software-Intensive Systems*, 2000. Online at http://ieeexplore.ieee.org/xpl/freeabs_all.jsp?isnumber=18957&arnumber=875998&count=1 (accessed September 5, 2007).

3. The Open Group. *The Open Group Architecture Framework, Frequently Asked Questions.* Online at http://www.opengroup.org/architecture/togaf8-doc/arch/toc.html (accessed September 5, 2007).

4. Ibid.

5. Dennis A. Stevenson. Presentation to the Department of Information Systems, University of Cape Town, June 1995. Online at <users.iafrica.com/o/om/omisditd/denniss/text/eapositn.html> (accessed October 11, 2006).

6. Ralph Whittle and Conrad B. Myrick. *Enterprise Business Architecture: The Formal Link between Strategy and Results*, 2005. Boca Raton, FL: CRC Press. Website highlighting the book is online at www.enterprisebusinessarchitecture.com/index.html (accessed September 2006).

7. Michael Kull and John Zachman. *Managing Integration in a Federated Architecture Environment,* 2003. The Intervista Institute, Inc. Online at http://www.intervista-institute.com/articles/zachman-by-kull.html (accessed September 2007).

8. The Open Group. "Developing a Business Architecture View," *TOGAF*™ *8.1.1 Online,* 2006. Online at www.opengroup.org/architecture/togaf 8-doc/arch/chap31.html#tag_32_08 (accessed October 11, 2006).

9. Ibid.

10. For more information on business modeling, visit the Business Process Management Initiative website at www.BPMI.org. The Business Process Management Initiative is an organization that defines standards for business process modeling, including the language used to specify business processes, their tasks/steps, and deliverables.

11. Scott Bittler. *Characteristics of an Effective Enterprise Architect,* 2005. META Group. Online at http://www.itworldcanada.com/Pages/Docbase/ ViewArticle.aspx?ID=idgml-3e21a390-4090-42f5-9279-23970f2ec7fe &Portal=1fa35bf9-d296-4571-8fff-c665a851ec1d&ParaStart=15&Para End=30&direction =prev&Previous=Previous (accessed April 18, 2006).

12. Ibid.

13. Dennis A. Stevenson. Presentation to the Department of Information Systems, University of Cape Town, June 1995. Online at <users.iafrica .com/o/om/omisditd/denniss/text/eapositn.html> (accessed October 11, 2006).

14. The Open Group. "Developing a Business Architecture View," *TOGAF*™ *8.1.1 Online,* 2006. Online at www.opengroup.org/architecture/togaf 8-doc/arch/chap31.html#tag_32_08 (accessed October 11, 2006).

15. The Chief Information Officers Council. *Federal Enterprise Architecture Framework*, Version 1.1, September 1999. Online at http://www.cio.gov/Documents/fedarch1.pdf (accessed September 2007).

16. John A. Zachman. *The Zachman Framework for Enterprise Architecture*, 1987. Pinckney, MI: The Zachman Institute for Framework Advancement. Online at http://www.zifa.com (accessed April 17, 2006).

17. Ibid.

18. Computer Science Corporation introduces its framework methodology on its website at http://www.csc.com/solutions/knowledgemanagement/mds/mds122/212.shtml (accessed September 2007).

Chapter 4

Using Feasibility Studies to Determine the Most Valuable Business Solution

In This Chapter:

- Defining the Feasibility Study

- Why Conduct a Feasibility Study?

- Conducting a Feasibility Study

- Challenges

- Best Practices

Organizations work hard to stay informed, analyze the most current information, and transform their businesses to keep pace with the rapidly changing competitive landscape. Business success depends on the ability to continually update and reinvent organizational thinking, analyze the current organizational state, and plan for the future. These challenges require innovative thought and a structured and deliberate business analysis process.

Strategic planning and the creation of a to-be business architecture provide a firm foundation for understanding where an organization is today and where it wants to be in the future. From this foundation, organizations must select the best initiatives to manage the changes necessary to reach goals as quickly as possible, and with the least cost and risk.

Defining the Feasibility Study

Feasibility studies are often used to crystallize new business opportunities, identify alternative solution options, and determine which options to pursue to reach organizational goals. Feasibility studies are fast becoming an essential business planning technique for executing strategy. The business analyst incorporates feasibility studies into the portfolio management process, making project selection more effective.

A feasibility study is an analysis effort that applies the disciplines of market research and statistical analysis to understand the competitive environment, enabling an organization to make sound decisions about improvements and new ventures. The most effective feasibility studies systematically collect and analyze data about the market—its trends and threats—to facilitate business decision-making. Feasibility studies use verifiable information and apply statistical measures to ensure a complete and accurate analysis.

A recent web search produced several definitions for *feasibility study*, revealing a variety of uses:[1]

+ A likelihood study. A way to determine if a business idea is capable of being achieved. The study asks, "Can it work and produce the level of profit necessary?"

+ A study of the applicability or practicability of a proposed action or plan.

+ An analysis of the business area to determine whether a system can cost-effectively support the business requirements.

+ A detailed investigation and analysis of a proposed development project to determine whether it is viable both technically and economically.

+ A study that determines if the information system makes sense for the organization from an economic and operational standpoint.

+ A market study and an economic analysis combined to provide an investor with knowledge about both the project environment and the project's expected return on investment.

+ An examination of a particular project or business to assess its chances of operating successfully, before committing large amounts of money to it.

+ An investigation into the economic environment, internal and external pressures, systems, procedures, and communication capability in a business area within a firm, to help corporate managers evaluate possible benefits of implementing a business or system change; an integral part of a corporate implementation plan.

These definitions all have a similar emphasis: feasibility studies consider a business problem or an opportunity and potential solutions *before* an implementation project is funded, to increase confidence in the project. Businesses spending millions of dollars on large-scale change initiatives every year are now realizing that a more rigorous analysis of the solution alternatives greatly increases the probability of a high return on project investments.

Why Conduct a Feasibility Study?

Most often, a feasibility study is commissioned to determine the viability of a new business opportunity. During strategic planning, executives may reference the information from feasibility studies to develop strategic plans, goals, and themes to achieve a future vision. During enterprise analysis, the portfolio management team may use feasibility studies to determine the best investment strategy needed to solve business problems and seize new business opportunities. During the requirements and design phases, feasibility studies may be used to help conduct tradeoff analysis among solution alternatives.

When formulating a major business transformation project (e.g., forming a new line of business, increasing market share through acquisition, developing a new product or service), feasibility studies greatly assist in identifying the vast array of alternative solutions. Lower-risk change initiatives usually require much more abbreviated studies.

The feasibility study is usually undertaken to add a more rigorous analysis methodology to solution options presented in the business case for proposed new initiatives. As a result, the business case and the feasibility study usually present similar information.

Conducting A Feasibility Study

Although the typical activities required to conduct a thorough feasibility study appear to be sequential, they are often conducted concurrently and iteratively; in some cases, certain steps can be omitted. The amount of rigor depends on the complexity, risk, and criticality of the effort. Typical steps include the following:

1. Determine the business drivers for the feasibility study.

2. Plan the feasibility study activities.

3. Define the current state of the organization and the competitive environment.

4. Identify solution options.

5. Analyze each solution option.

6. Prepare feasibility study reports.

Determine the Business Drivers for the Feasibility Study

Feasibility studies are used to help determine the optimum solution for various business initiatives. Businesses undertake major change initiatives either to solve a *business problem* or to take advantage of a *business opportunity*. Enterprise analysis activities may identify a business problem or a business opportunity. A business problem typically emerges from business operations. For example, a particular business process may be failing to meet certain expectations.

In other cases, a new business opportunity identified during strategic planning and goal setting may appropriately lead to a study to determine whether pursuing the opportunity would be a wise venture economically, technologically, and operationally. A business opportunity could be introducing a new product or service, or expanding to create a new line of business.

Commissioning a Feasibility Study to Solve a Business Problem

Typical steps in determining whether to commission a feasibility study to solve a business problem include the following:

+ Identify the sponsor who is shepherding (and likely funding) the study.

+ Document the problem in as much detail as possible.

+ Determine any adverse impacts the problem is causing within the organization, and quantify those impacts (e.g., potential lost revenue, inefficiencies).

+ Determine how quickly the problem could potentially be resolved, and the cost of doing nothing.

+ Conduct a root cause analysis to determine the underlying source of the problem.

- Determine the potential areas of investment required to address the problem.

- Draft a requirements statement describing the business need for a solution to the problem.

- Determine the potential areas of investment required to address the problem (e.g., business process reengineering, acquisition of an existing business, new and improved technology).

- Determine the methodology or approach needed to complete the feasibility study.

- Determine the resources required and time needed to complete the study.

- Propose the study to an appropriate sponsor.

Commissioning a Feasibility Study to Take Advantage of a Business Opportunity

Typical steps in determining whether to commission a feasibility study to exploit a business opportunity include the following:

- Identify the sponsor who is shepherding (and likely funding) the study.

- Define the opportunity in as much detail as possible, including the events that led up to the discovery of the opportunity, and the business benefits expected if the opportunity is pursued.

- Quantify the expected benefits in terms (e.g., increased revenue, reduced costs).

- Determine how quickly the business opportunity could be exploited and the cost of doing nothing.

+ Determine the cost of pursuing this opportunity.

+ Determine the methodology or approach needed to complete the feasibility study.

+ Determine the potential areas of investment required to address the situation (e.g., business process reengineering, acquisition of an existing business, new and improved technology).

+ Draft a requirements statement describing the business need for pursuing the opportunity.

+ Determine the resources required and time needed to complete the study.

+ Propose the study to the appropriate sponsor.

Plan the Feasibility Study Activities

As the business analyst embarks upon the effort to plan and execute the feasibility study, it is wise to first build a core team of subject matter experts (SMEs) to serve as a study team. Planning and executing a major feasibility study requires a wide range of skills and techniques that the business analyst might not possess. As a result, it's best to enlist a team of experts who pay strong attention to detail, as well as provide business architecture skills, research and statistical analysis skills, business and technical writing skills, leadership, organization, and team-building skills, adaptability and change management skills, and communications skills. A strong, relevant knowledge of the industry and the organizational vision, mission, strategic goals, and organizational policies and procedures are also important, as is a broad understanding of the technology that supports the business.

Having a well-rounded team with requisite skills and knowledge ensures that the data gathered and analysis conducted represent the collective wisdom of both experienced business and technology professionals. Core team members typically include:

+ *Project manager*—Even though a project manager isn't assigned until after a project is officially commissioned, it's important to consult an experienced project manager to help develop the project scope and to prepare time and cost estimates.

+ *Business visionary*—Involve a business SME who is a creative thinker and a futurist, one who represents the business area under consideration. This SME will help identify and evaluate the solution options and determine the best approach among feasible alternatives, determine business boundaries for the change initiative, and forecast the business benefits expected from the project outcome.

+ *Chief technologist*—Involve a technology SME who is a visionary and advocate of advanced technology to achieve a competitive advantage. This SME will help craft technically feasible alternative solution options, determine the best option, and estimate the cost of acquiring or building the solution.

+ *Financial Analyst*—Involve a senior financial analyst to help prepare a cost/benefit analysis to demonstrate the economic viability of the proposed project.

After assembling a core study team, begin planning the feasibility study by determining the decision criteria used to formulate options for consideration, evaluate those options, and determine the business objectives the solution must satisfy. At this point the study team conducts typical planning steps:

+ Start with the end in mind. Determine the format for the feasibility study report. It is important to define the scope and contents of the report during the planning stage to ensure that all of the most important information will be generated during the study.

+ Identify and document all activities needed to complete the feasibility study.

+ Review work-to-date with the sponsor to validate that the study requirements, plans, objectives, benefit criteria, and evaluation measures will meet the business need.

Define the Current State of the Organization and the Competitive Environment

The study team conducts an internal current-state analysis, as well as an external competitive analysis, as the first step of the actual feasibility study. This analysis may include a review of the current business architecture, including information about business objectives, strategy, and vision, an analysis of current business processes, and/or an assessment of future business architecture documentation. The current-state assessment typically considers the following elements, depending on the nature and scope of the study:

+ The business vision, strategy, goals, and measures

+ The objectives of each line of business that has a stake in the area under study (collect relevant organization charts)

+ The physical location of each impacted line of business

+ The major types of business information required

+ Current relevant business applications and supporting technologies, including technology architecture diagrams depicting the interfaces between current business technologies

♦ Current (relevant) business processes, including process flow diagrams depicting the flow of process steps needed to complete a business function

Defining the current state is expedited if business architectural components for the current state of the organization are already complete and up-to-date. If this is not the case, the documentation developed during the current-state assessment can serve as a basis for developing the business architecture. Most of the techniques used to develop the business architecture are applicable to current-state assessments prior to the feasibility study.

The study team conducts an analysis of the external business environment, including a competitive analysis, an analysis of market trends and emerging markets, new and emerging technologies, and recent changes in the regulatory environment. The study team also conducts external research about the potential opportunity or business problem to uncover industry-specific information, industry benchmarks, risks, and results of similar attempts implemented by others.

Identify Solution Options

After defining the internal current state of the organization and the external competitive environment, the study team identifies potential solutions that could meet the business objectives. During this stage, the business analyst conducts frequent brainstorming sessions with the study team and any additional SMEs who may add value to the discovery session. This is the most creative portion of the feasibility study. Don't worry if there is a certain amount of chaos and churn during this creative stage, because it stimulates creative thinking. The most innovative solutions are also likely to be the most complex; allow the group to spend some time at the edge of chaos.

It is important for the business analyst to create an environment that stimulates originality and focuses on future possibilities to identify the most creative solutions. Persons with a predetermined bias toward a certain solution should probably not be invited to participate in this portion of the study, to prevent undue influence over the final recommendations.

Analyze Each Solution Option

Once all potential solution options have been identified, the group of experts transitions from brainstorming to analysis. Each solution option is analyzed for economic, technical, operational, cultural, and legal feasibility. The benefits, costs, risks, issues, assumptions, and constraints associated with each solution option are described in detail and compared against other options to determine the most viable solution.

Solution Feasibility

Describe the feasibility of each solution option—in both the business and technical environments—by indicating the resource requirements, costs, assumptions, constraints, risks, business outcomes, and business benefits for each of three phases: (1) building or acquiring the solution option, (2) implementing the solution option, and (3) operating the solution option.

Numerous techniques help in assessing the feasibility of each option, including:

+ Market surveys that prove current market acceptance and to forecast demand

+ Technology advancement analysis to examine the latest technical capabilities, and to ensure the solution is not beyond the current limits of technology

+ COTS (commercial off-the-shelf) software package compare/ contrast analysis

- Business staff interviews to determine operational feasibility in the workplace

- IT staff interviews to determine operational feasibility in the technical operating environment

- Finance staff and project manager interviews to ensure economic feasibility

- Prototype projects to build a component of the proposed solution to prove that (at least) high-risk components of the proposed solution are technically feasible

- Risk identification, assessment, ranking, and response planning

- Benchmark analysis to determine best-in-class practices

- Competitive analysis to examine the potential market success of the solution

- Environmental impact analysis

- Early cost versus benefit analysis (which will be covered in more detail under the task to develop the business case)

- Issue identification, assessment, ranking, and response planning

Typically, analysis matrices or logs are used to capture the results of the feasibility analysis. The same type and level of information is documented for each solution option. See Figure 4-1 for a summary solution feasibility analysis log.

Figure 4-1—Summary Level Solution Feasibility Analysis Log

Category	Building/ Acquiring the Solution	Implementing the Solution	Operating the Solution
Resources			
Costs			
Assumptions			
Constraints			
Risks			
Outcomes			
Benefits			

Subsidiary analysis logs may also be developed to provide the rationale for the estimates provided in the summary-level log presented in Figure 4-1.

Solution Benefits

Describe any tangible (e.g., quantifiable in terms of cost savings or increased revenue) and intangible benefits (e.g., employee morale or customer satisfaction) to the organization that may result if the solution option is implemented. The estimates provided by the feasibility study are intended to be preliminary; estimates become more precise when completing the business case. Figure 4-2 presents a sample solution benefits log. As you can see, there may be numerous benefit categories.

Figure 4-2—Solution Benefits Log

Benefit Category	Benefit	Value	Estimating Assumptions
Financial	• New revenue generated • Reduction in costs • Increased profit margin		
Operational	• Improved operational efficiency • Reduction in product time-to-market • Enhanced quality of product/service		
Market	• Increased market awareness • Greater market share • Additional competitive advantage		
Customer	• Improved customer satisfaction • Increased customer retention • Greater customer loyalty		
Staff	• Increased staff satisfaction • Increased staff retention • Improved organizational culture		

Solution Costs

Describe any tangible and intangible costs to the organization that may result if the solution option is implemented. Include the costs of the actual project (e.g., equipment procured); and include any negative impact caused by the delivery of the project (e.g., operational down-time).

Here again, the estimates provided by the feasibility study are preliminary; estimates become more precise when completing the business case. Figure 4-3 presents a sample solution costs log. Note that the log includes value/year, (e.g., increased revenue each year) versus value one time, (e.g., a one time cost saving from the sale of a facility).

Figure 4-3—Solution Costs Log

Category	Cost	Value / Year	Value One Time
People	• Project staff salaries • Contractors/outsourced parties • Training courses		
Physical	• Building premises for project team • Equipment and materials • Tools (e.g., computers, phones)		
Marketing	• Advertising/branding • Promotional materials • Public relations and communications		
Organizational	• Operational down-time • Short-term loss in productivity • Cultural change		

Solution Risks

Solution risks describe the most apparent risks to the organization if the solution option is implemented. Risks may be strategic, cultural, environmental, financial, operational, technical, industrial, competitive, or customer-related. Figure 4-4 presents a sample solution risks log.

Figure 4-4—Solution Risks Log

Risk Item # Description	Probability	Impact	Status	Owner	Date	Risk Response Strategy
1.						
2.						
3.						

Solution Issues

Finally, solution issues describe any high-priority issues associated with this solution option. An *issue* is an identified event that will likely adversely affect the ability of the solution to produce required deliverables. Figure 4-5 presents a sample solution issues log.

Figure 4-5—Solution Issues Log

Issue ID#	Issue Name/ Description	Status	Owner	Date Due	Action Plan/ Resolution	Date Closed

Solution Assumptions and Constraints

Assumptions help to fill gaps in information; they describe information that is assumed to be true, but can not be validated (e.g., a required skillset is readily available). Constraints describe any major limitations to the solution's implementation (e.g., a standard technical platform).

Determine the Most Viable Solution

The expert team then reviews all of the feasibility data about each potential solution option and determines the best alternative. If there is no clear best option, the business analyst facilitates the expert team to arrive at a consensus on the alternative solution to recommend to the sponsor. The team identifies additional criteria and reviews it to distinguish between the options. The team then shares the results of the feasibility studies with the sponsor for approval to proceed with analysis activities that build a business case for a recommended solution.

Prepare Feasibility Study Reports

All of the information captured during the feasibility study is collected in a report that identifies each of the solution options available and rates each option's likelihood of achieving the desired results. The Appendixes section offers a template feasibility study report, as well as more formal templates for the risk, issue, and decision logs that can be used to document any study team decisions.

- An executive summary

- A statement defining the business problem or opportunity, including the requirement statement describing the business need for either a solution to the problem or for pursuing the opportunity

- Decision criteria used to formulate options for consideration

- Information gathered during the current-state analysis and during the analysis of the greater competitive environment

- A list of solution options

- The feasibility analysis results for each solution option, including:

  - A complete description of the solution option

  - A complete description of the assessment process and methodology

  - A list of benefits provided by the solution option

  - A list of costs to the organization

- A list of identified risks associated with the solution option

- A list of identified issues that, once the solution option is implemented, could adversely impact the success of the solution

- A description of any major assumptions and/or constraints associated with this solution option

- An alternative solution ranking, including the ranking criteria and scores for each option (Appendix F offers a project ranking tool template)

- The study results, including the recommended solution and any rationale for the decision

- An appendix containing all supporting documentation (e.g., analysis logs)

Additional information in the report may include:

- The solution option's strategic ties to the organization's strategy, direction, and mission

- The solution option's technological alignment with the organization's current architecture standards.

- The availability of COTS (commercial off-the-shelf) software packages

- The extent to which existing business solutions will change

As the practice of portfolio management matures in business organizations, there will be a greater need to conduct feasibility studies for large-scale change initiatives. Conducting this kind of rigorous analysis provides a great deal of insight into the likelihood of project success prior to the authorization of funds. However, few organizations are investing in rigorous enterprise analysis prior to project approval, likely due to the challenges cited below.

Challenges

Common barriers to the successful completion of feasibility studies include the following:

- Difficulty in securing sponsorship for the feasibility study

- Cultural resistance: "It is not the way we do things around here."

- Incomplete business architecture components; they are necessary to complete the current-state assessment

- Lack of process to fund or resource studies of this magnitude

- Insufficient time is allotted for the study

- Insufficient knowledge by the study team about feasibility studies, and lack of skills needed to plan and conduct a meaningful study

Best Practices

As feasibility studies become more prevalent, best practices have been identified to conduct them successfully:

- Use both qualitative and quantitative analysis to compare the organization to others in the same industry, and to compare various solution options

- Use standard scientific investigative research practices

- Compare and contrast various elements of the study

- Use proven quality-enhancing techniques (e.g., Six Sigma).

As we have discovered, the practice of conducting feasibility studies prior to making significant investments can serve a company well. World-class organizations are conducting detailed market investigations and feasibility studies of a proposed project to determine whether an identified solution can cost effectively support business requirements. Once the feasibility study is complete, the team goes on to create the business case (discussed in detail in the next chapter) that provides the investment governance group (the portfolio management team) with knowledge of both the environment where the project exists and the expected return on investment to be derived from it.

Endnotes

1. Referenced websites include: U.S. Small Business Association (http://www .sba.gov/library/sbaglossary.html#F); Bureau of Justice Assistance, Center for Program Analysis (http://www.ojp.usdoj.gov/BJA/evaluation/ glossary/glossary_f.htm); Webopedia (http://www.webopedia.com/ TERM/S/SSADM.html); Massachusetts Executive Office of Energy and Environmental Affairs (http://commpres.env.state.ma.us/content/ glossary.asp); and the Oregon Innovation Center (www.oregoninnovation .org/pressroom/glossary.d-f.html).

Chapter 5

Preparing the Business Case and Decision Package

In This Chapter:

- Assemble a Core Team
- Decide on a Recommended Option
- Think Strategically
- Identify and Confirm a Project Sponsor
- Determine the Project Scope
- Conduct a Cost-Benefit Analysis
- Conduct the Initial Risk Assessment
- Draft the Business Case
- Prepare the Final Decision Package
- Challenges
- Best Practices

A *business case* is a structured proposal for business improvement that describes a proposed new change initiative in enough detail that the portfolio management team can determine whether to invest in the effort. If a feasibility study has been conducted, the business case includes or references information from the study. Whether or not a feasibility study has been conducted, the business case includes a description of the business problem or opportunity, a list of the solution options, the costs and benefits associated with each solution option, and a recommended solution option with rationale. It's also important to stress the strategic alignment of the solution option, including how the solution supports the organization's strategies; if the solution sets priorities inconsistent with the organization's strategies, include the rationale for considering the investment and any contingency plans to address those risks.[1]

Although not all companies require a business case for major project investments, the practice is becoming more prevalent among organizations attempting to implement strategic portfolio management techniques for project selection and prioritization. The business case, supporting information from feasibility studies, the business architecture, and other business planning and analysis documents are combined into a *decision package* and presented to the portfolio management team for a decision.

The following sections discuss the activities that are typically used to create a business case. Many organizations do not conduct formal feasibility studies and so incorporate some feasibility activities and analysis into the business case. Therefore, some of the feasibility activities discussed in the previous chapter are reiterated here as necessary components of the business case.

Assemble a Core Team

The business analyst assembles and collaborates with a core team of highly skilled and experienced subject matter experts (SMEs) to provide expert judgment in analyzing the solution options and assembling the decision package for the portfolio management team. This is necessary because of the wide range of knowledge, skills, and techniques needed to prepare the complete decision package. Table 5-1 presents a list of the qualities needed to be successful.

Table 5-1—Knowledge, Skills, and Techniques Used to Prepare the Decision Package

Knowledge, Skills, and Techniques Used to Prepare the Decision Package	
• Project planning, estimating, and scheduling techniques • Organizational change readiness and management techniques • Financial cost-benefit models • Structured problem solving techniques • Data-gathering and research approaches • Modeling techniques including entity relationship diagrams, process diagrams, and workflow diagrams	• Scope definition and decomposition • Risk contingency and mitigation techniques • Root-cause analysis • Tradeoff analysis • Risk identification and analysis • Probability and impact analysis • Structured decision analysis

Core team members typically include:

+ *Project manager*—Even though a project manager isn't assigned until after a project is officially commissioned, it's important to consult an experienced project manager to help develop the project scope and to prepare time and cost estimates.

+ *Business visionary*—Involve a business SME who is a creative thinker and futurist, one who represents the business area under consideration. This SME will help identify and evaluate the solution options and determine the best approach among feasible alternatives, determine business boundaries for the change initiative, and forecast the business benefits expected from the project outcome.

+ *Chief technologist*—Involve a technology SME who is a visionary and advocate of advanced technology to achieve a competitive advantage. This SME will help craft technically feasible alternative solution options, determine the best option, and estimate the cost of acquiring or building the solution.

+ *Financial Analyst*—Involve a senior financial analyst to help prepare a cost/benefit analysis to demonstrate the economic viability of the proposed project.

Decide on a Recommended Option

After assembling the core team, decide on the recommended solution option—the proposed project. As discussed in Chapter 4, for major changes it is prudent to undertake a formal feasibility study. This process involves thoroughly assessing the current business problem or opportunity, identifying the various solution options available, determining the likelihood of successful implementation for each solution option, and selecting the recommended solution option. If a formal feasibility study has not been conducted, the business case development team will need to conduct a similar analysis (refer to Chapter 4 for details).

Think Strategically

Once the team assembles and confirms a recommended solution option, consider that solution option—now becoming a proposed project—in its wider context. How will the proposed new business solution offer value through the organization to its customers more effectively and efficiently? How does the proposed project solution fit into the greater strategy of the organization; how does it support an existing competitive advantage or create a new one?[2]

Thinking strategically involves the following steps:

+ Describe the big picture. Identify the type of business strategy the proposed project supports. Be aware of how other projects contribute to the organizational business strategies, and how this proposed project will fit into the project portfolio.

+ Determine how the proposed project will promote this strategy.

- Determine how the proposed project will sustain the organization's competitive advantage.

- Define how fulfilling the plans and objectives outlined in the business case for this project will implement the strategy.

- Determine ways to link the numbers (in terms of reduced cost and/or increased revenue) in the business case to the strategy and to the strategic scorecard, if one exists.

Identify and Confirm a Project Business Sponsor

The business sponsor usually asks a senior business analyst or a member of senior management to prepare the business case. If the proposed project is approved it is the business sponsor who provides the financial resources for the project, dedicates business representatives to participate in the project, and is accountable for the business benefits expected from project outcomes.

Determine the Project Scope

Begin to draft the business case by summarizing information collected to date, including the competitive assessment results, the current-state and industry environment analyses, the business problem or opportunity, the solution options considered, the recommended solution, and the rationale for its selection.

After drafting this summary, define the project scope, which includes describing the project objectives, determining expected high-level deliverables (e.g., products, services), documenting business and project assumptions and constraints, and building a high-level statement of the anticipated work effort. First draft the preliminary scope statement, including:

- In-scope and out-of-scope essentials

- Preliminary product scope statement, including a high-level description of the desired product, service, or outcome

- High-level work breakdown structure (WBS), used to estimate cost and schedule (decomposed to level 2 or 3)

- Project boundaries in terms of business processes and process owners

- IT systems depicted in context or business domain models, or other diagrams to define the boundaries of the proposed project

- The initial list of stakeholders

- The impact of the proposed project on the business operations, as well as on the technology infrastructure

- The initial cost, time, and resource requirement estimates based on the WBS

- The most likely solution development approach, (e.g., partitioning the proposed project into sequential releases, developing in-house, purchasing the solution)

After drafting the relevant project scope information, a cost-benefit analysis is elaborated further, ideally with the assistance of a professional financial analyst to help prepare economic models and forecasts.

Conduct a Cost-Benefit Analysis

After defining the scope of the proposed project, the core team works to determine its economic viability. Previous feasibility analyses should have provided initial information about the economic, operational, and technical feasibility of the recommended option. The core team now builds on that information, drafting the case to justify the proposed project solution in terms of the value it will add to the business, and compares that value to the estimated costs to develop, purchase, and/or operate the solution.

It is important to support the cost and benefit estimates with information on the methods, assumptions, and rationale used to quantify them. It is also important to predict costs and business benefits in terms that will be measurable after the solution is delivered. Only then can the enterprise determine the return on its project investments.

Defining Costs

Calculating the *total cost of ownership* (TCO) helps the portfolio management team understand the budgeted (direct) and unbudgeted (indirect) costs associated with the proposed project and solution. This cost represents the total cost to both purchase or develop the solution, and to own and operate the solution throughout its useful life, which includes related business and technical operations, training, upgrades, and administration. The TCO may also include any opportunity costs associated with *not* choosing to invest in other solution options, and any costs related to changes to organizational work practices.

Defining Benefits

Describe expected qualitative and quantitative business benefits to demonstrate how the project solution is intended to achieve business objectives and promote strategic advantages (e.g., by reducing costs, increasing revenue, improving market share). Benefits may be projected in terms of:

- Expected market penetration

- Estimates of cost and time to break even

+ Profit expectations

+ Follow-on opportunities

+ Expected cash flow consequences of the action over time

Challenges Associated with Cost-Benefit Analyses

Preparing cost estimates during this enterprise analysis, pre-project phase is often problematic for large projects with a significant IT component. IT projects have historically had a high level of uncertainty, and they require greater efforts to define the solution before it is possible to estimate costs and benefits with a high degree of confidence. It is simply not possible to accurately predict the cost of large projects at this stage, before more detailed planning and analysis activities have taken place.

Preliminary cost estimates can and should be used to help distinguish between alternative solution options. But a common problem occurs when senior managers—who must make a decision to invest at this stage—tend to insist the figures presented in these early forecasts remain fixed throughout the project life cycle. It is essential to emphasize the uncertain nature of these early forecasts in all discussions with the project sponsor.

Underlying many of the problems associated with developing and realizing business case projections is the immature measurement culture within many organizations today. The business case should present not just projected benefits, for example, but also benefit assessment and evaluation methodologies. This may include information about needed developments of internal measures or systems to ensure that the benefits predicted in the business case can be observed, measured, and evaluated.

Conduct the Initial Risk Assessment

The analysis activities to prepare the business case are not complete until an initial risk assessment is performed. Although this initial risk assessment is performed as a component of enterprise analysis activities, most of the risk management processes are repeated throughout the project. *Project risk* is defined as an uncertain event or condition that, if it occurs, has a positive or negative effect on at least one project objective, such as time, cost, scope, or quality. *Project risk management* includes conducting risk management planning, identification, analysis, response, and monitoring and control on a project.[3]

The purpose of the initial risk assessment is twofold: (1) to determine whether the proposed project carries more risk than the organization is willing to bear, and (2) to adjust the cost and benefit projections on the basis of the risks identified at this point. The business analyst facilitates members of the core team to conduct the risk assessment, including the following process steps:

+ Risk identification

+ Risk assessment

+ Risk response planning

+ Organizational readiness assessment

+ Risk avoidance

+ Risk rating

+ Benefit adjustments

Risk Identification

This process yields the best results when conducted as a creative brainstorming session. The goal is to identify business, financial, technical, and operational risks. This process answers the following questions:

+ What are the risks that the project will exceed cost and schedule estimates significantly?

+ What are the risks that the solution will not completely resolve the business problem?

+ What are the risks that the solution will not realize the estimated benefits?

+ What are the risks that the solution will exceed estimated costs to operate it in the business environment? In the technical environment?

+ What are the technical risks that might impact cost or performance?

Risk Assessment

For each identified risk, assess the probability that it will occur, and the impact if it does occur (usually assessed using *high, medium,* and *low* indicators). To do this, the business analyst or project manager facilitates a discussion of each risk item to arrive at a consensus on the probability and impact ratings. Once ratings are established for probability and impact, the team determines an overall rating for the risk item.

Risk Response Planning

For high-probability and/or high-impact risks, the business analyst or project manager facilitates a discussion to identify risk response plans, assess the cost of these plans, and add these costs to the overall project cost forecast. Reassess the probability and impact of each risk to ensure the responses reduce the probability or impact.

Organizational Readiness Assessment

Assess the organizational readiness and capacity for the changes that will be brought about by the proposed project. If the change is significant, the costs—in terms of training, retooling, new-staff acquisition, and overcoming the cultural resistance to change—could be considerable. Be sure to include these costs into the economic forecasts.

Risk Avoidance

Describe the risk of doing nothing—taking no action to solve the business problem or to take advantage of the new business opportunity. Be sure to include the cost of doing nothing (not solving the business problem or not taking advantage of the new opportunity) in the business case.

Risk Rating

Calculate an overall risk rating for the proposed project in terms of the costs, time, and solution quality. This answers the question, "What are the risks associated with actually realizing the projected business benefits described in the business case?" The business analyst facilitates a discussion to determine just how risky the proposed project is considered to be, and includes this information in the business case. The portfolio management team may be willing to take the risk if the reward is great, or the proposed project may pose more risk than the organization is willing to take.

Benefit Adjustments

If the risk assessment activities uncover high-priority risks to achieving the business benefits, it may be appropriate to adjust the benefit forecasts and take another look at the risk-adjusted cost/benefit ratio.

Draft the Business Case

The business case is the key document used by the portfolio management team to approve and prioritize projects. See Appendix A for a business case document template. Typical elements of the business case document and supporting information include:

- Executive summary

- Business problem and/or opportunity description

- A summary of the internal and environmental assessment

- Identified solution options

  - Option 1: description, benefits, costs, feasibility, risks, issues, assumptions, and constraints

  - Option 2: description, benefits, costs, feasibility, risks, issues, assumptions, and constraints

  - Option n... and so on for each option

- Recommended option and rationale

- Most likely implementation approach (e.g., build or buy)

- Appendix: supporting information provided as an appendix or referenced as relating documents

  - Strategic plans, goals, themes, measures

- Current and future-state business architecture, if available

- The complete benchmark studies, competitive analyses, and feasibility studies, if available

After completing the business case, the business analyst meets with the sponsor and presents the key points in an informal meeting. The sponsor decides whether the proposed project proceeds forward to the portfolio management team for consideration. If the sponsor agrees to propose the project, the business analyst prepares the final decision package for the portfolio management team.

Prepare the Final Decision Package

The business analyst prepares an executive briefing for the project sponsor, and then compiles all relevant project information into a formal collection that functions as a decision package for the portfolio management team.

Challenges

The challenges the business analyst faces when preparing the decision package for the project sponsor to present to the portfolio management team include the following:

- Business architecture components for the business area under consideration do not exist; thus, extra time is required to develop the architecture to some degree to complete the current-state assessment.

- There is insufficient time and/or funding allotted to conduct an appropriate level of pre-project enterprise analysis.

- The business analyst is unable to bring together a core group of SMEs with adequate knowledge and skills to complete the required activities.

- The portfolio management team is not yet mature enough to use the decision package optimally to make project selection decisions (e.g., they lack the process, tools, and discipline to make decisions; they lack a strategic perspective about investments).

- The project sponsor is not available to participate in developing, reviewing, and approving the decision package.

- The level of detail presented to the portfolio management team is inappropriate, providing too little or too much information to enable the team to make the best decisions.

- Information in the decision package doesn't clearly present the value a proposed project is expected to bring to the organization.

Best Practices

As with most key business analysis activities, the use of standards, rigor, and a disciplined process will consistently yield a quality outcome. Best practices for preparing the decision package for new project proposals include the following:

- Use standard project management practices to scope the proposed project

- Assemble a small core group of SMEs to conduct the analysis

- Estimate costs using a WBS decomposed to level 3

- Estimate schedules using historical information

- Use standard cost/benefit and break-even economic models

- Prepare the feasibility study and business case documents using a standard template

+ Use a business case template that requires expected project outcomes to align with organizational vision and strategic goals.

Endnotes

1. Dennis J. Cohen and Robert J. Graham. *The Project Manager's MBA*, 2001. San Francisco, CA: Jossey-Bass.

2. Ibid.

3. The Project Management Institute. *A Guide to the Project Management Body of Knowledge*, 3rd ed., 2004. Newtown Square, PA: The Project Management Institute, Inc.

Chapter 6

Managing Projects for Value

In This Chapter:

- Enhancing Portfolio Management Practices in Organizations

- Validating the Business Case throughout the Business Solution Life Cycle

- Measuring the Business Value of Solution Features

- Measuring the Business Value after Solution Delivery

Previous chapters have discussed the role of the business analyst in strategic planning and goal setting, portfolio management practices designed to execute strategy through valuable programs and supporting projects, and providing decision-support information to the portfolio management governance group. These tasks involve creating and maintaining the business architecture; conducting feasibility studies to identify solution options; identifying, scoping, defining, and preparing the business case for new business opportunities; conducting initial risk assessments for new business opportunities; and preparing the decision package for project proposals.

As rigorous as these business analysis practices appear, they are comparatively easy because they are essentially forecasting and planning techniques. Now the enterprise must use various portfolio management practices to act on the information gathered during these studies. Let's review how the portfolio management practice works in organizations and then how the business analyst keeps his or her eye on the business benefits throughout the project cycle.

Enhancing Portfolio Management Practices in Organizations

Sound business analysis is needed to make effective, strategic decisions. In his book *Good to Great,* author Jim Collins writes that although entrepreneurial success is fueled by creativity, imagination, and the spirit to move into unknown territories, it also risks chaos as a company grows and complexity increases.[1] A culture of discipline, Collins claims, is needed as employees, customers, products, and transactions increase and problems arise: "Everyone would like to be the best, but most organizations lack the discipline to figure out with egoless clarity what they can be best at and the will to do whatever it takes to turn that potential into reality."[2]

It is time for organizations to impose some professional management practices for making portfolio investment decisions. Effective portfolio management processes allow for both freedom and responsibility within a decision framework. Under the leadership and guidance of senior business analysts, portfolio management provides the discipline to make strategic decisions that facilitate organizational potential, and it provides the framework to act on the decisions.

Senior business analysts and project managers work to design and implement a streamlined, efficient, non-bureaucratic portfolio management process and toolset for their organizations. The sponsor of the proposed project presents information in summary form to the portfolio management governance group, typically using an executive briefing and a complete decision package, as discussed in Chapter 5.

Using project selection and prioritization tools, the portfolio management governance group determines the priority of the proposed project. Refer to Figure 2-9 and Appendix F for sample project ranking tools.

The portfolio management group compares proposed projects to the list of current, funded, and active projects, as well as to the list of backlogged projects, to determine where it fits in the organization's project portfolio. If the proposed project is of higher priority than other funded projects, the group decides to either defer existing projects to reallocate resources to the new, higher-priority opportunity, or fund this new project, securing additional resources as necessary. If the proposed project is of lower priority than other funded projects, the group inserts the new project into the backlog list in order of priority.

Validating the Business Case throughout the Business Solution Life Cycle

In many organizations, the portfolio management process stops after the project is selected, prioritized, and approved for funding. To protect this investment, however, it is important to manage the value of the project throughout its lifecycle—and here again, the business analyst plays a critical role.

During the life of the project, the business analyst continually reviews and updates the business case. Most organizations conduct some sort of phase-end review (also called stage-gate review or control-gate review) for large projects. In preparation for each phase-end review, the project team updates detailed project plans and re-plans the next major phase. At the same time, the business analyst updates the business case with current cost, schedule, risk, and benefit estimates to determine whether the business case is still valid and whether the project still warrants continued investment.

After updating the project plans, the project manager, business analyst, project business representative and lead developer collaborate to present a consensus recommendation regarding continued investment in the project. The business analyst often attends management review meetings and helps present the current status of the project and recommendations for future investment. Three basic investment recommendations include:

+ Terminate the project because the costs or the risks associated with achieving the business benefits are too high

+ Redirect the project, reducing the scope of the solution or changing course altogether

+ Continue to invest in the project because it still appears to be a viable investment that will bring significant benefits to the organization

Projects are often difficult to terminate; even major course corrections can be difficult. When the investment has been significant, executives and managers often must continue regardless of results. Many consider it a failure to cancel a project, because it essentially admits that the decision to proceed with the project was wrong or that the project was not managed well. However, world-class organizations keep a close eye on their large project portfolio investments and make adjustments along the way as necessary, just as individuals do with their personal financial investment portfolios.

Measuring the Business Value of Solution Features

The business analyst uses the business case as a guide to elicit, analyze, document, validate, and manage requirements for the new project solution throughout the business solution life cycle (BSLC). The business analyst documents the requirements in increments, each increment containing a set of functions or features, and collaborates with the project manager to conduct a cost-benefit analysis for each feature. The team then prioritizes each increment according to its projected value to the organization, and compares it to the information contained in the business case to ensure priorities align with strategies.

Measuring Business Value After Solution Delivery

During the BSLC, the business analyst plays a vital role in ensuring that metrics and measurements are put into place to track any return on project investment (ROI), often for several months or years after project completion. When the solution is in the operations and maintenance phase of the BSLC, the business analyst reviews and analyzes metrics and measures to determine whether the project outcomes delivered the business benefits forecasted in the business case, and whether the operating costs for the new solution align to original forecasts. Only then can the portfolio management team truly know if it made a sound investment.

If a project fails to realize its forecasted ROI, the business analyst should conduct further analysis to continuously improve the project portfolio management process. For example, a root-cause analysis can determine what circumstances prohibited project outcomes from delivering their expected value to the organization.

Possible reasons a project fails to realize its projected ROI include:

+ The investment was not sound, likely because the economic forecasts in the business case were inaccurate or incomplete (e.g., many organizations do not include total cost of ownership in their cost estimates, as discussed earlier).

+ The project team executed the project poorly, resulting in schedule and cost overruns.

+ The solution was not implemented optimally in the business environment, thus reducing its benefits to the organization.

We have examined the emerging and critical role of the business analyst to help organizations achieve strategic goals through programs and supporting projects. Business analysts provide decision-support information to the leadership team so they can establish a future vision, set strategic goals, select the most valuable projects, and then execute them flawlessly. As the role of the business analyst evolves and matures, senior business analysts will emerge as the key individuals in the organization that have the business and technical prowess to facilitate a process to execute strategy. In the next chapter we will examine the evolution from business analyst to business strategist.

Endnotes

1. Jim Collins. *Good to Great*, 2001. New York: Harper Business.

2. Ibid.

Chapter 7

Evolving from Business Analyst to Business Strategist

In This Chapter:

- Self-education

- Professional Associations

- Experience

- Training and Accreditation

- Mentoring

Sometimes it is tempting—and even necessary—to invest heavily in IT-enabled business processes designed merely to sustain the business. However, while some of these investments are necessary or even critical, investing only in continuous sustenance is a failing business strategy. The current fast-changing business environment requires that a much larger portion of investments in projects be aimed at innovation and business growth. It is through *value-based portfolio management* that organizations are unlocking the value of business improvement and IT investments.

Senior business analysts play a critical role in the portfolio management process. Indeed, it would be difficult to overstate the value of business analysts to businesses today. According to Brenda Kerton, a senior research analyst with Info-Tech Research Group,

"Several factors have converged to create the perfect storm for BAs who will see increased salaries and increased demand for their skills. Experienced BAs will get more difficult to find."[1]

The question is, how can analysts, who are often seen as IT resources, transition into senior business analysts serving their organizations as internal business/technology consultants? According to a 2006 survey by *CIO Magazine*, 55 percent of IT executives plan to increase their IT staff by an average of 11 percent, and roles in the highest demand combine business and technological expertise—the emerging role of the business analyst.[2]

To increase your ability to represent both IT and business perspectives, you can explore several avenues of professional development, including:

* Self-education

* Professional associations

* Experience

* Training and accreditation

* Mentoring

Self-education

The most successful people find time to focus on their professional development. Become passionate about your work and continually update your knowledge to stay current. An array of articles, books, and conferences addressing the subjects of portfolio management, business analysis, and business transformation best practices are coming to the fore. Industry conferences, for example, include:

* Project Summit and Business Analyst World

+ Project World and the World Congress for Business Analysis

+ PMI Global Congress

Industry conferences not only provide an opportunity to transfer knowledge, they are also beneficial for their networking opportunities. Aggressively pursue building a strong network of business analysis professionals.

Although the role of the business analyst is foremost a business-related role, the more you know about IT, the more value you will provide to your organization. The growing maturity of IT practices is important because IT management and governance are now increasingly critical to organization strategic success: IT best practices are crucial in establishing effective information governance. These IT best practices have become significant as organizations demand better returns from IT investments. Organizations must strategically align their IT projects to deliver value through project outcomes. They can do this by managing risk, resources, and performance, and by introducing improvements in business efficiency to gain trust from business partners and respect from customers.

Professional Associations

In addition to professional development through self-study, educate yourself on the many organizations and institutes dedicated to the advancement of best practices for IT-enabled business solutions, including the following:

+ The Systems and Software Consortium, or SSCI, provides industry and government the insight, advice, and tools needed to help them address the complex and dynamic world of software and systems development. For more information, refer to the website www.software.org.

- The IT Governance Institute, or ITGI™, was founded in 1998 to advance international thinking and standards in directing and controlling IT groups to ensure that IT supports business goals, optimizes business investment in IT, and appropriately manages IT-related risks and opportunities. Also from ITGI™, the Control Objectives for Information and Related Technology (COBIT®) provides a comprehensive framework for managing and delivering high-quality IT-based services. For more information, refer to the website www.itgi.org.

- IT Infrastructure Library (ITIL), Version 2, and IT Service Management (ITSM) document best practices for IT service management. For more information about these resources and for information about IT transformation, refer to the websites www.itil-itsm-world.com and www.itsm.info/home.htm.

- The Project Management Institute, long acknowledged as a pioneer in the field of project management, has a truly global membership of more than 200,000 professionals representing 125 countries. PMI offers certification for project management professionals (PMPs). For more information, refer to the website www.pmi.org.

- The recently formed International Institute for Business Analysis is the leading worldwide professional association that develops and maintains standards for the practice of business analysis and for the certification of practitioners. The IIBA offers certification for business analysis professionals (CBAP). For more information, refer to the website www.theiiba.org.

Experience

There is no substitute for experience! Self-education, professional associations, and certifications alone cannot replace the value of lessons learned. As organizations continue to improve their portfolio management processes, there will be a critical shortage of highly seasoned business analysts and project managers to lead strategic projects. So don't waste a moment. Jump in head first and seek out assignments to learn the craft.

Training and Accreditation

Impressive professional business analysis training programs are available. Look for leading-edge courses that focus on increased performance, best practices, and project results. The courses should be based on sound systems engineering principles, focus on leadership and facilitation skills, be rich in lean-thinking and agile tool sets, and be filled with tailoring techniques for small, medium, and large, high-risk projects.

Seek out course offerings that are designed to provide practical guidelines and skills that lead to immediate results for writing, defining, analyzing, and managing IT-enabled business solutions requirements. They should be based on real-world experiences and case studies, and offer practical strategies, well-tested methods, and tools for implementing requirements management techniques.

Mentoring

Searching for and building a strong relationship with a mentor is one of the most rewarding and valuable strategies toward advancing your career. The mentor should be a senior professional in your organization who understands the critical needs of business-focused, IT-enabled projects. Aligning yourself with senior and more experienced business and/or IT professionals will expose you to an array of information, tools, techniques, and best practices learned and successfully applied throughout the mentor's career.

Consulting a mentor not only exposes you to more senior members of the organization, but it can also increase project performance, helping the organization realize its expected return on project investments. Additional benefits include:

+ Increased confidence and motivation

+ Effective and efficient approaches to business analysis

+ Opportunities to use tools and practice techniques

+ Protected feedback, i.e., "no-risk" reviews

+ Networking through access to other professionals

+ Access to information and best practices

+ Support to ensure successful project performance

So there you have it. The journey from business analyst to business strategist is a fulfilling and challenging ride. Don't hesitate to take it—if you blink, you may miss the career of a lifetime!

Endnotes

1. Brenda Kerton. *Analyst Role Is In Demand*, 2006. Toronto: Info-Tech Research Group.

2. Edward Prewitt and Lorraine Cosgrove Ware. "The State of the CIO, Survey '06," *CIO Magazine*, 2006. Online at http://www.cio.com/archive/010106/JAN1SOC.pdf (accessed September 2007).

Appendixes

Appendix A:
Business Case Template

Appendix B:
Feasibility Study Template

Appendix C:
Issues Log Template

Appendix D:
Decision Log Template

Appendix E:
Risk Log Template

Appendix F:
Project Ranking Template

Appendix A

Business Case Template

Business Case

For

[Project Name]

Prepared by:

Date:

Version:

Document Control

	Information
Document ID	[Document Management System #]
Document Owner	[Owner Name]
Issue Date	[Date]
Last Saved Date	[Date]
File Name	[Name]

Version	Issue Date	Changes
[1.0]	[Date]	[Section, Page(s) and Text Revised]

Approvals

Role	Name	Signature	Date
Project Sponsor			
Portfolio Management Chairperson			
Project Office Director			
Business Analyst			
Project Manager			
CIO			
CFO			

Table of Contents

The Business Case Document

The Purpose of the Business Case

The business case is the document that links project proposals to strategic business goals. The business case describes significant, high-risk project proposals by weighing the investment against its potential business value. Business analysts complete the business case after developing strategic goals and themes and before selecting and funding projects. The business case captures information needed to effectively propose investment in a new project.

The business case justifies the application of resources to a proposed initiative. Significant resources are needed for large, complex, strategic projects. The business case serves as a financial anchor to ensure companies do not commit significant investments on the basis of inadequate decision-support information.

What Is a Business Case?

A well-formed business case is:

+ A business-oriented tool that supports sound project investment decisions

+ A proposal to invest in a change initiative

+ A formally structured argument for taking a course of action

+ A trigger to secure project funding

The Benefits of Using a Business Case

A well-formed business case provides organizations with the following benefits:

+ It verifies the strategic alignment of project objectives

+ It drives consensus decision-making among executives

+ It ensures a common understanding about the project among stakeholders

+ It supports risk management practices

+ It imposes a disciplined approach to the decision-making process that requires the consideration of all relevant factors

Who Prepares the Business Case?

Authors of the business case can vary widely across organizations. However, basic roles should include the following:

+ Lead author: senior business analyst or manager

+ Supporting authors: subject matter experts enlisted by the lead author to participate in the business analysis activities (e.g., project manager, IT manager, business visionary, financial analyst, researchers)

+ Key stakeholders: those who are likely to be impacted by the initiative

Steps to Prepare the Business Case

The basic steps needed to complete the business case may vary somewhat, but a general list is given below. If a feasibility study was conducted, the process starts at step 6; a standard feasibility study report captures the information gathered from steps 1 through 5.

1. Characterize the business problem or new opportunity

2. Conduct a quick current state and competitive assessment

3. Identify solution options

4. Conduct an analysis of the feasibility of each option

5. Review recommended option(s) with the executive sponsor

6. Determine the proposed project's boundaries and scope

7. Conduct cost/benefit analysis

8. Conduct initial risk assessment

9. Create the business case

How to Use This Template

This document provides a guide to completing a business case. Add, remove, or redefine sections to meet unique business requirements. Example tables, diagrams, and charts are included to provide further guidance on how to complete each section.

Executive Summary

Summarize information and findings from each sections by briefly describing the:

+ Problem or opportunity

+ Solution alternatives

+ Recommended solution

+ Implementation approach

The Business Case

Describe the business case document, why and how it was developed, and for whom it was prepared.

Current Business Situation

Describe the current state of the business, including problems and opportunities, and their origin and nature. Provide information about the importance of the initiative to the organization, and elements that would characterize a successful outcome.

Environmental Analysis

Describe the business drivers and the core aspects of the business environment that have triggered the need for this project. These may include:

+ Business vision, strategy, strategic themes

+ Insufficient business processes or technologies

+ New competitor products or processes

+ New technology trends (or opportunities resulting from new technologies)

+ Commercial or operational trends driving changes in the business

+ Changes to regulatory, legislative, or other legal requirements

Provide any facts or evidence to support these conclusions.

Opportunity Analysis

Describe the business problem or new business opportunity. If the project is meant to solve a business problem, describe the following:

+ Document the problem in as much detail as possible

+ Determine the adverse impacts the problem is causing within the organization, and quantify the impacts as much as possible (e.g., lost revenue, inefficiencies)

+ Determine the immediacy of the resolution and the cost of doing nothing

+ Conduct a root-cause analysis to determine the underlying source of the issues

+ Determine the potential areas of study required to address the issues

+ Draft a requirements statement describing the business need for a solution

If the project is being proposed to take advantage of a new business opportunity, describe the following:

+ Define the opportunity in as much detail as possible, including the events that led up to the discovery of the opportunity and the business benefits the opportunity could potentially offer

+ Quantify the expected benefits as much as possible (e.g., increased revenue, reduced costs)

+ Determine the immediacy of the opportunity and the cost of doing nothing

+ Identify the cost of pursuing this opportunity versus the costs of other opportunities

+ Determine the potential areas of study required to understand the viability of the opportunity, and determine the methodology or approach needed to complete the study

+ Draft a requirements statement describing any business needs related to the opportunity

Alternative Assessment

This section provides a qualitative and quantitative evaluation, analysis, and comparison of all feasible solution options. Options suggested may include doing nothing, doing something that will achieve a similar result, or doing something that will achieve a better result than current performance. If a feasibility study was conducted, it will have already provided this information for each option. Provide the following information for each solution option:

Option 1 — [Option Name]
Description

Provide a detailed description of the solution option.

Feasibility Analysis

Describe the feasibility of the solution option by indicating the resource requirements, costs, assumptions, constraints, risks, business outcomes, and business benefits for three phases: building or acquiring the solution option, implementing the solution option, and operating the solution option. Be sure to include information about the solution operations in both the business and technical environments.

	Building/ acquiring the solution	Implementing the solution	Operating the solution
Resources			
Costs			
Assumptions			
Constraints			

	Building/ acquiring the solution	Implementing the solution	Operating the solution
Risks			
Outcomes			
Benefits			

Summary of Changes Required

To summarize the overall feasibility of this solution option, break the solution down into components and rate the feasibility of each component in the following table:

New Business Assets	# Required	Method Used to Determine Feasibility
New technology		A technology prototype was created to assess the solution
New people		A survey was completed to identify skillset availability
New processes		Processes within similar organizations were reviewed
New facilities		Physical assets were inspected
Other		

Benefits

Describe the tangible and intangible benefits to the company upon implementation of the solution. One obvious benefit is that the solution will address the business problem or opportunity outlined above. The benefits given below are examples only. Actual performance figures must support all quantifiable benefits after the solution is operational.

Category	Benefit	Value	Assumptions
Financial	• New revenue generated • Reduction in costs • Increased profit margin	$ x $ x $ x	
Operational	• Improved operational efficiency • Reduction in product time to market • Enhanced quality of product/service	x % x hrs x %	
Market	• Increased market awareness • Greater market share • Additional competitive advantage	x % x % Describe	
Customer	• Improved customer satisfaction • Increased customer retention • Greater customer loyalty	x % x % Describe	
Staff	• Increased staff satisfaction • Improved organizational culture • Longer staff retention	x % Describe x %	

Costs

Describe the estimated tangible and intangible costs to the company if the solution option is implemented. Include the costs of the actual project (e.g., procured equipment), as well as any negative impact to the business resulting from the delivery of the project (e.g., operational downtime).

Category	Cost	Value per Year	Value One Time	Budgeted
People	• Salaries of project staff • Contractors, outsourced parties • Training courses	$ x $ x $ x	$ x $ x $ x	Yes No Yes
Physical	• Building premises for project team • Equipment and materials • Tools (e.g., computers, phones)	$ x $ x $ x	$ x $ x $ x	No No No

Category	Cost	Value per Year	Value One Time	Budgeted
Marketing	• Advertising, branding • Promotional materials • PR and communications	$ x $ x $ x	$ x $ x $ x	Yes No No
Organizational	• Operational downtime • Short-term loss in productivity • Cultural change	$ x $ x Describe	$ x $ x Describe	No No No

You may need to identify whether the cost item is a capital or operational expenditure. Attach a separate spreadsheet showing an analysis of the cost equations as an appendix to this document if further information is needed for approval.

Risks

Summarize the most apparent risks associated with this solution option. Risks may be strategic, cultural, environmental, financial, operational, technical, industrial, competitive, or customer-related.

Risk Item Description	Probability	Impact	Status	Owner	Date	Risk Response Strategy

To complete this section thoroughly, it may be necessary to undertake a formal risk assessment by documenting a risk management plan. Define clear mitigation techniques or plans to reduce the likelihood and impact of each risk.

Issues

Summarize the highest priority issues associated with the adoption of this solution option. Issues are events that adversely affect the ability of the solution option to produce the required deliverables.

Issue ID#	Issue Name/ Description	Status	Owner	Date Due	Action Plan/ Resolution	Date Closed
1.						
2.						
3.						

Assumptions and Constraints

List the major assumptions and constraints associated with the adoption of this solution option.

Summary, Conclusion, and Recommendations

Summarize the entire business case at a high level, revisit findings and conclusions, and close with recommendations.

Option Rankings

Identify the criteria by which each of the solution options was assessed. Then assign a rating for each criterion to determine a total score for each option.

Solution Option Selection Criteria	Weight (W)	Initial Rating [R]	Final Rating [W * R]
Customer Satisfaction 1--10 Low High			
Strategic Alignment 1--10 Low High			
Employee Satisfaction 1--10 Low High			
Increased Revenue 1--10 Low High			
Reduced Cost 1--10 Low High			
Longevity 1--10 Short – Long – Use for 2 Yrs Use 4+ Yrs			
Size of Investment 10--1 Small—$25–100K Large— >$100K 6 Months 12 Months			
Project Complexity Risk 10--1 Relatively Simple Relatively Complex Straightforward Poorly Understood			
New Technology Risk 10--1 Proven S/W H/W Unproven S/W H/W			
Benefit Risk 10--1 Known Committed Risky Benefits Out-Year Estimates			
TOTAL RATING			

Legend:

1. *Customer Satisfaction*: impact of project on external customers
2. *Business Results*: impact of project on strategic goals
3. *Employee Satisfaction*: impact of project on employee retention
4. *Revenue*: impact of project on increased revenue
5. *Cost*: low versus high cost to fund the project
6. *Longevity*: length of time the enterprise will benefit from the new product or service
7. *Size of Investment*: large versus small investment risk
8. *Project Complexity Risk*: simple versus complex project
9. *New Technology Risk*: proven technology versus cutting edge/unproven
10. *Benefit Risk*: risk to realizing projected benefits

Option Recommended

Based primarily on the highest total score achieved above, choose the recommended option for approval. Summarize the primary reasons why this option was chosen over other options.

Implementation Approach

Provide an overview of the general approach undertaken to deliver the preferred solution option and derive the business benefits.

Attachments

Supporting Documentation

Attach any documentation relevant to the business case. For example:

+ Problem/opportunity research materials

+ Feasibility study research materials

+ External quotes or tenders

+ Detailed cost/benefit spreadsheets

+ Other relevant information or correspondence

Appendix B

Feasibility Study Template

Feasibility Study

For

[Project Name]

Prepared by:

Date:

Version:

Document Control

	Information
Document ID	*[Document Management System #]*
Document Owner	*[Owner Name]*
Issue Date	*[Date]*
Last Saved Date	*[Date]*
File Name	*[Name]*

Version	**Issue Date**	**Changes**
[1.0]	*[Date]*	*[Section, Page(s) and Text Revised]*

Approvals

Role	**Name**	**Signature**	**Date**
Project Sponsor			
Portfolio Management Chairperson			
Project Office Director			
Business Analyst			
Project Manager			
CIO			
CFO			

Table of Contents

The Feasibility Study

The Purpose of the Feasibility Study

Feasibility studies are analysis efforts that apply the disciplines of market research and statistical analysis to understand the competitive environment, enabling organizations to make sound decisions about improvements and new ventures. Formal feasibility studies involve a systematic collection and analysis of data about the market and its preferences, opinions, trends, and plans used for corporate decision making. In practice, feasibility studies use verifiable information and apply statistical measures to ensure a complete and accurate analysis of the information gathered.

When do I use a Feasibility Study?

Feasibility studies are often used to crystallize new business opportunities or solve a business problem, identify alternative solution options to close the gap between the current and future state of the business, and to determine the best solution option to pursue in any of these cases.

Most often, a feasibility study is commissioned to determine the viability of an idea for a new business opportunity. In the strategic planning phase of the business solution life cycle (BSLC), feasibility studies may provide information to the strategic planning process when executives are developing strategic plans, goals, and themes to achieve the future vision.

In the enterprise analysis phase of the BSLC, feasibility studies are often used to help the portfolio management team determine the best investment path to solve business problems and seize new business opportunities. During the requirements and design phases of the BSLC, feasibility studies may be used to help conduct trade-off analysis among solution alternatives.

Steps to Prepare the Feasibility Study

The basic steps to complete a feasibility study may vary somewhat, but in general they are as follows:

1. Determine the business drivers for the study: either a business problem or a new business opportunity

2. Plan the feasibility study effort

3. Determine the current state of the enterprise

4. Determine solution options

5. Conduct a feasibility analysis for each option

6. Prepare a feasibility study report

Who Prepares the Feasibility Study Report?

Authors of the feasibility study report can vary widely across organizations. However, basic roles should include the following:

+ Lead author: senior business analyst or manager

+ Supporting authors: subject matter experts enlisted by the lead author to participate in the business analysis activities (e.g., project manager, IT manager, business visionary, financial analyst, researchers)

+ Key stakeholders: those who are likely to be impacted by the initiative

How to Use This Template

This document provides a guide on the topics usually included in a feasibility study report. Add, remove, or redefine sections as necessary to meet your particular business circumstances. Example tables, diagrams, and charts are included to provide further guidance on how to complete each relevant section.

Executive Summary

Summarize information and findings from each of the sections in this document.

Business Problem or Opportunity

Current State of the Enterprise and the Competitive Environment

Describe the business environment in terms of all or part of these elements, depending on the nature and scope of the study:

+ The business vision, strategy, goals, and measures

+ The objectives of each business unit that has a stake in the area under study, and collect relevant organizational charts

+ The physical location of each impacted business unit

+ The major types of business information required

+ Current business technology

+ Current business processes relevant to this project

+ The current business environment, including a competitive analysis, an analysis of market trends and emerging markets, new and emerging technologies, and recent changes in the regulatory environment

The Business Problem or Opportunity

Describe the business problem or new business opportunity. If the study has been commissioned to solve a business problem, reports typically include the following information:

- ✦ Document the problem in as much detail as possible.

- ✦ Determine the adverse impacts the problem is causing within the organization, and quantify the impacts in terms of lost revenue, inefficiencies, etc.

- ✦ Determine the immediacy of the resolution and the cost of doing nothing.

- ✦ Conduct a root-cause analysis to determine the underlying source of the issues.

- ✦ Determine the potential areas of study required to address the issues.

- ✦ Draft a requirements statement describing the business need for a solution.

If the study has been commissioned to take advantage of a new business opportunity, reports typically include the following information:

- ✦ Define the opportunity in as much detail as possible, including the events that led up to the discovery of the opportunity and the business benefits expected if the opportunity is pursued.

- ✦ Quantify the expected benefits in terms of increased revenue, reduced costs, etc.

- ✦ Determine the immediacy of the resolution and the cost of doing nothing.

+ Identify the opportunity cost of pursuing this opportunity versus another under consideration.

+ Determine the methodology or approach planned to conduct the study.

+ Determine the potential areas of study required to understand the viability of the opportunity.

+ Draft a requirements statement describing the business need for a solution.

Feasibility Study Process

Study Team Members

List members of the study team, and their subject matter expertise.

Name	Role	Subject Matter Expertise
	Study team lead	Business analysis
	Executive sponsor	Business unit vision and challenges
	Study team member	Financial analysis
	Study team member	Project management

Describe the process used by the study team to complete the feasibility study, including:

+ Decision criteria used to evaluate alternative solution options

+ Business objectives the solution must satisfy

+ Activities performed to complete the study

+ Deliverable(s) produced

+ Executive sponsor involvement

Solution Evaluation Criteria

Provide a list of the criteria used to evaluate the feasibility of each solution option.

Feasibility Study Methods

List the methods used to determine the feasibility of each option. Possible techniques include:

+ Market surveys to prove acceptance and to forecast demand in the marketplace

+ Technology feasibility assessment to ensure the solution is not beyond the current limits of technology

+ Interviews

   □ Business staff interviews to determine operational feasibility in the workplace

   □ IT staff interviews to determine operational feasibility in the technical operating environment

   □ Finance staff and project manager interviews to estimate the cost of the solution option to ensure economic feasibility

+ Prototyping to build a component of the proposed solution to prove that the highest-risk components of the proposed solution are technically feasible

+ Risk identification, assessment, ranking, and response planning, captured in a risk log

- Benchmarking analysis to determine best-in-class practices

- Competitive analysis to examine the viability of market success

- Environmental impact analysis

- Technology advancement analysis to examine the latest technical approaches to solving the business problem

- Early cost/benefit analysis (covered in greater detail in the business case)

- Comparative analysis for a COTS package

- Issue identification, assessment, ranking, and response planning, captured in an issues log

Solution Options

List all solution options that could potentially meet the objectives identified in the planning process; always include the option of doing nothing. Assess the likelihood of each option meeting the requirements. In addition, define the risks, issues, assumptions, and constraints associated with the feasibility of each option. Document the results as follows.

Alternatives Assessment

This section provides a qualitative and quantitative evaluation, analysis, and comparison of all feasible options. Options suggested may include doing nothing, doing something that will achieve a result similar to current performance, or doing something that will achieve a better result than current performance. Include the following information for each solution option:

Option 1 — [Solution Option Name]
Description

Provide a detailed description of the option.

Feasibility Analysis

Describe the feasibility of the solution option by indicating the resource requirements, costs, assumptions, constraints, risks, business outcomes, and business benefits for the three phases: building or acquiring the solution option, implementing the solution option, and operating the solution option. Be sure to include information about the feasibility of the solution operations in both the business and technical environments.

	Building/acquiring the solution	Implementing the solution	Operating the solution
Resources			
Costs			
Assumptions			
Constraints			
Risks			
Outcomes			
Benefits			

Benefits

Describe the tangible and intangible benefits to the company expected upon implementation of the solution. One obvious benefit is that the solution will address the business problem or opportunity outlined above. The benefits given below are preliminary and will become more precise when writing the business case.

Category	Benefit	Value	Assumptions
Financial	• New revenue generated • Reduction in costs • Increased profit margin		
Operational	• Improved operational efficiency • Reduction in product time to market • Enhanced quality of product/service		
Market	• Increased market awareness • Greater market share • Additional competitive advantage		
Customer	• Improved customer satisfaction • Increased customer retention • Greater customer loyalty		
Staff	• Increased staff satisfaction • Improved organizational culture • Longer staff retention		

Costs

Describe the tangible and intangible costs to the company upon implementation of the solution. Include the costs of the actual project (e.g., procured equipment), as well as any negative impact to the business resulting from the delivery of the project (e.g., operational down time). The estimates given below are preliminary and will become more precise when writing the business case.

Category	Cost	Value per Year	Value One Time	Budgeted
People	• Salaries of project staff • Contractors, outsourced parties • Training courses	$ x $ x $ x	$ x $ x $ x	Yes No Yes
Physical	• Building premises for project team • Equipment and materials • Tools (e.g., computers, phones)	$ x $ x $ x	$ x $ x $ x	No No No
Marketing	• Advertising, branding • Promotional materials • PR and communications	$ x $ x $ x	$ x $ x $ x	Yes No No
Organizational	• Operational down time • Short-term loss in productivity • Cultural change	$ x $ x Describe	$ x $ x Describe	No No No

Risks

Summarize the most apparent risks associated with this solution option. Risks may be strategic, cultural, environmental, financial, operational, technical, industrial, competitive, or customer-related.

Risk Item Description	Probability	Impact	Status	Owner	Date	Risk Response Strategy

To complete this section thoroughly, it may be necessary to undertake a formal risk assessment by documenting a risk management plan. Define clear mitigation techniques or plans to reduce the likelihood and impact of each risk.

Issues

Summarize the highest priority issues associated with the adoption of this solution option. Issues are events that adversely affect the ability of the solution option to produce the required deliverables.

Issue ID#	Issue Name/ Description	Status	Owner	Date Due	Action Plan/ Resolution	Date Closed
1.						
2.						
3.						

Assumptions and Constraints

List the major assumptions and constraints associated with the adoption of this solution option.

Summary, Conclusion, and Recommendations

Summarize the entire business case at a high level, revisit findings and conclusions, and close with recommendations.

Option Rankings

Identify the criteria by which each of the solution options was assessed. Then assign a rating for each criterion to determine a total score for each option.

Solution Option Selection Criteria	Weight (W)	Initial Rating [R]	Final Rating [W * R]
Customer Satisfaction 1----------10 Low High			
Strategic Alignment 1----------10 Low High			
Employee Satisfaction 1----------10 Low High			
Increased Revenue 1----------10 Low High			
Reduced Cost 1----------10 Low High			
Longevity 1----------10 Short – Use for 2 Yrs Long – Use 4+ Yrs			
Size of Investment 10----------1 Small—$25–100K 6 Months Large— >$100K 12 Months			
Project Complexity Risk 10----------1 Relatively Simple Straightforward Relatively Complex Poorly Understood			
New Technology Risk 10----------1 Proven S/W H/W Unproven S/W H/W			
Benefit Risk 10----------1 Known Committed Benefits Risky Out-Year Estimates			
TOTAL RATING			

Legend:

1. *Customer Satisfaction*: impact of project on external customers
2. *Business Results*: impact of project on strategic goals
3. *Employee Satisfaction*: impact of project on employee retention
4. *Revenue*: impact of project on increased revenue
5. *Cost*: low versus high cost to fund the project
6. *Longevity*: length of time the enterprise will benefit from the new product or service
7. *Size of Investment*: large versus small investment risk
8. *Project Complexity Risk*: simple versus complex project
9. *New Technology Risk*: proven technology versus cutting edge/unproven
10. *Benefit Risk*: risk to realizing projected benefits

Option Recommended

Based primarily on the highest total score achieved above, choose the recommended option for approval. Summarize the primary reasons why this option was chosen over other options.

Implementation Approach

Provide an overview of the general approach undertaken to deliver the preferred solution option and derive the business benefits.

Attachments

Supporting Documentation

Attach any documentation relevant to the business case. For example:

- Problem/opportunity research materials

- Feasibility study research materials

- External quotes or tenders

- Detailed cost/benefit spreadsheets

- Other relevant information or correspondence

Appendix C

Issues Log Template

Feasibility Study Information			
Study Name:		Project ID#:	
Study Lead:		As-of Date:	
Study Team Members:			

Issues Log

Issue ID#	Issue Name/ Description	Status	Owner	Date Due	Action Plan/ Resolution	Date Closed
1.						
2.						
3.						

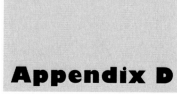

Appendix D

Decision Log Template

Feasibility Study Information			
Study Name:		Project ID#:	
Study Lead:		As-of Date:	
Study Team Members:			

Decision Log

Decision ID#	Decision	Status	Owner	Date Made	Context/ Rationale	Comments

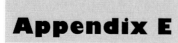

Appendix E

Risk Log Template

Feasibility Study Information			
Study Name:		Project ID#:	
Study Lead:		As-of Date:	
Study Team Members:			

Risk Log

Risk Item Description	Probability	Impact	Status	Owner	Date	Risk Response Strategy

Appendix F

Project Ranking Template

Purpose

To convert corporate strategies into project selection criteria, and to rate the criteria according to importance, i.e., according to their influence in achieving strategic goals.

Description

The project selection criteria are developed as an outgrowth of the Strategic Planning Process. Anytime the corporate strategy changes, the project selection criteria must be reviewed and perhaps refined.

How to Use this Form

The Portfolio Planning and Management Team uses this tool to establish a relative ranking of a project. In addition, it will be used to continually to review and refine project priorities as business needs change and innovative concepts emerge. The worksheet will be used when evaluating:

1. New project proposals

2. Solution option analysis

3. Programs and projects during program reviews.

Project Information	
Project Name:	
Submitted by:	
Date Submitted:	
Date Ranked:	
Ranking:	

Project Summary	
Objectives:	
Costs:	
Benefits:	
Major Deliverables:	
Date Needed:	
Summary Description:	

Solution Option Selection Criteria	Weight (W)	Initial Rating [R]	Final Rating [W * R]
Customer Satisfaction 1------------------------------10 Low　　　　　　　　High			
Strategic Alignment 1------------------------------10 Low　　　　　　　　High			
Employee Satisfaction 1------------------------------10 Low　　　　　　　　High			
Increased Revenue 1------------------------------10 Low　　　　　　　　High			
Reduced Cost 1------------------------------10 Low　　　　　　　　High			
Longevity 1------------------------------10 Short –　　　　　　Long – Use for 2 Yrs　　　Use 4+ Yrs			
Size of Investment 10------------------------------1 Small—$25–100K　　Large— >$100K 6 Months　　　　　12 Months			
Project Complexity Risk 10------------------------------1 Relatively Simple　　Relatively Complex Straightforward　　　Poorly Understood			
New Technology Risk 10------------------------------1 Proven S/W H/W　　Unproven S/W H/W			
Benefit Risk 10------------------------------1 Known Committed　　　　　Risky Benefits　　　　　Out-Year Estimates			
TOTAL RATING			

Legend:

1. *Customer Satisfaction*: impact of project on external customers
2. *Business Results*: impact of project on strategic goals
3. *Employee Satisfaction*: impact of project on employee retention
4. *Revenue*: impact of project on increased revenue
5. *Cost*: low versus high cost to fund the project
6. *Longevity*: length of time the enterprise will benefit from the new product or service
7. *Size of Investment*: large versus small investment risk
8. *Project Complexity Risk*: simple versus complex project
9. *New Technology Risk*: proven technology versus cutting edge/unproven
10. *Benefit Risk*: risk to realizing projected benefits

Index